D1392944

Towards Equality

Towards Equality

A Christian Manifesto

BOB HOLMAN

First published in Great Britain 1997
Society for Promoting Christian Knowledge
Holy Trinity Church
Marylebone Road
London NW1 4DU

Biblical quotations are from
The Revised English Bible © 1989 Oxford and Cambridge
University Presses

British Library Cataloguing-in-Publication Data

A catalogue record of this book is available from
the British Library

ISBN 0-281-05046-5

Typeset by Pioneer Associates, Perthshire
Printed in Great Britain by
The Cromwell Press, Melksham, Wiltshire

To
Bron Soan

Contents

Preface

Britain displays all kinds of inequalities, those between different ethnic groups, between men and women, between people with special needs and others. In this book, I say little about them. Living in Easterhouse, Glasgow, I daily come across wider inequalities, those social and material disadvantages which affect whole sections of the population in the same society in which other sections enjoy opulence and advantage. This kind of inequality is the theme of this book.

As a Christian, I am convinced that the Bible (and the version used here is *The Revised English Bible*) reveals a God who did not intend his creation to be marred by gross inequality. As a former academic and, for the last twenty years, a neighbourhood worker, I have perceived how inequality frequently spoils the lives of God's creatures. I therefore urge Christians to promote greater equality.

I realize that in Britain many people follow a religion other than Christianity and that others have no religious faith. However, I hope they will find in the following pages some arguments which make a case for equality whatever their religious beliefs.

Today inequality is not only widespread, it is also widely accepted. Those who advocate equality are going against the social tide and are not likely to be winners in the popularity stakes. Therefore I wish to thank Naomi Starkey of SPCK for her enthusiasm about publishing this book. My strongest thanks, as always, go to my wife, Annette, who supports me financially sometimes, prayerfully often and emotionally always.

Bob Holman

1

The Christian Case for Equality

The rich man in his castle,
The poor man at his gate,
God made them high and lowly,
And ordered their estate.

This verse, written by Mrs C. F. Alexander in 1848 in her hymn,
'All things bright and beautiful' reveals an acceptance of the
position of poverty as God-given. To be sure, as Stephen Mayor
has demonstrated, there were Christian contemporaries of Mrs
Alexander who regarded poverty more as the gift of the devil
(1967). None the less, it is true to say that the prevailing mood of
church members was that riches and poverty were as much a part
of the divine order as the existence of lords and labourers. Today
the churches are not quite so accepting. The well-known report
of the Archbishop of Canterbury's Commission on Urban
Priority Areas, *Faith in the City*, roundly condemned the existence
of poverty within modern Britain and called upon readers 'to
stand more closely alongside the risen Christ with those who are
poor and powerless' (1985, p. 360). In the 1990s, not only the
Archbishop of Canterbury but also leaders of many other denominations call upon the government to tackle homelessness, low
incomes, despair. Perhaps even more effectively, the Christian
organization, Church Action Against Poverty, has enabled poor
citizens themselves to articulate their plight.

Poverty Today

The definition and meaning of poverty is still a matter of debate.
There are those who, like Sir Keith Joseph and Jonathan

Sumption, say that a family is poor only if it cannot afford to eat (1979). This is to regard human beings as little more than animals whose needs are met if they are fed, watered and sheltered. Happily most commentators now regard them as social creatures who also have social, emotional and intellectual needs. Further, it is widely accepted that poverty is a relative concept, that is, it changes as standards of what is or is not acceptable for human decency alter. For instance, during the Second World War, as an evacuee, I lived in a number of houses which did not have an indoor toilet, one which did not have indoor water. This was not considered exceptional but today, when the vast majority of homes have an indoor toilet, to be without one would be regarded as being socially deprived.

Three definitions of poverty now have some support.

- The Benefits Poverty Level. In the United Kingdom, successive governments have assumed that the basic level of state financial support – be it called National Assistance, Supplementary Benefit or Income Support – is the poverty line. In 1965, Brian Abel-Smith and Peter Townsend published a study, *The Poor and the Poorest*, which threw doubts on the sufficiency of this measure. Professor Townsend, who became the most prominent British writer on poverty, thereafter produced further studies to argue that the line was set far too low and individuals with incomes below 120 per cent or 140 per cent of the prevailing rates were in real hardship. Taking 140 per cent of Income Support as the level, in the early 1990s some 18,540,000 were living on or below the margins of poverty. This is 33 per cent of the population as compared with 14 per cent in 1979.

- The Basic Essentials Level stems from a survey conducted by London Weekend TV for its series entitled *Breadline Britain*. Joanna Mack and Stewart Lansley explain that the objective of its approach was to discover whether there was any agreement in the country as to what constituted a minimum standard of living (1985). The researchers asked a representative sample to choose from a list of items those they regarded as essential. There was remarkable agreement about such items as damp-free housing, an inside toilet, a waterproof coat, heating for living rooms, an annual holiday and so on. People lacking three or more essential items were graded as poor. The estimated number in Britain in

1985 was 7.5 million. By 1990 it had risen to 11 million, that is 20 per cent of the population.

- Households Below Half Average Income. This measure is used throughout the European Community. In 1979 in the United Kingdom, the number of people with incomes below half the national average (after housing costs) was 5 million. By 1990 it was 13.5 million, that is, nearly a quarter of the population.

Whatever measure is used, it is clear that poverty is both extensive and increasing.

I need no convincing about the reality of poverty. I have been in the world of welfare for over thirty years and I can state that it is in the last few years more than in any others that I have met residents who are, at times, without food or money. For the last decade I have lived and worked on the huge Glasgow housing scheme of Easterhouse where over 70 per cent of school children qualify for clothing grants, that is, they come from families with very low incomes. Working for a neighbourhood project, I kept an analysis over a three and a half year period of sixty-five families (or individuals) who called at our flat on 757 occasions for a definite form of help. Their problems or needs were categorized as follows.

Problem	Number	Per cent
Money	237	31.3
Practical needs	180	23.7
Child care difficulties	97	12.8
Welfare rights advice	73	9.6
Personal problems	71	9.3
Health worries	67	8.8
Victims of crime	19	2.5
Other	13	1.7

Money problems included not being able to pay bills, being in the hands of loan sharks, wanting money for an electricity power card or just penniless. Practical needs encompassed people wanting a second-hand pram or cooker, asking where they could get the hoover mended cheaply, or a boy asking, 'Can Mum borrow two tea bags until Monday?' Welfare rights advice was to do with neighbours asking for advice on whether they could appeal when their application for a Social Fund loan was rejected, what to do about a letter threatening eviction, or questions as to the meaning of baffling terminology in official forms. If these three categories are taken together, then over 64 per cent of the callers came with difficulties stemming from poverty (B. Holman, 1997).

I see poverty nearly every day of my life and, along with many other Christians, I need no convincing that it is morally wrong and that Christians are fully justified in calling for its alleviation.

Equality

Yet the problem is not just poverty. I know many people who are poor, but often they do not like to be called poor or socially deprived. I called on a neighbour whose son had put his name down for one of our club holidays and explained that it cost only £15 as it was subsidized by Children in Need. The mother refused to let him go, 'We're not in need, we don't want a subsidy, we don't want charity, treat us the same as everybody else.' She was implying, 'We want equal treatment.' I went into the home of a middle-aged woman who has battled hard to bring up her children in a damp flat with little money. She was at a low ebb, 'I can't go on', she sobbed, 'It's not fair, some have got so much and I've got so little.' She perceived rightly that her problems were part of an unequal society.

Recently, I received a phone call at 11.45 p.m. asking for help. A family, who had lived at the bottom of our street, had to move when their building was demolished. The council put them into a nearby flat which was in much better condition but was infested with drug dealers. The parents – good parents much concerned about their children – persuaded the council to transfer them again and this time they went to another part of Glasgow; but here they were almost immediately set upon by a local mob and hence the call to me. As I drove them back to Easterhouse, the father looked wistfully at some of the large, safe, private houses and asked, 'Why can't we be like that?' In essence, these friends of mine were aggrieved not just that they had low incomes and poor conditions, but that they had them alongside those who had money in abundance. They considered gross inequalities to be unfair and wanted greater equality.

But the views and wishes of the residents of places such as Easterhouse count for little. Equality has gone out of fashion. In

1988, Margaret Drabble, after explaining that 'egalitarianism is that which asserts equality', stated, 'Twenty years ago, a profession of faith in egalitarianism was not considered improper or eccentric. It is now. By some shift of usage, by some change in the climate of thought, egalitarianism has become a dirty word, a devalued word' (1988, p. 1).

In 1995 Lord Dahrendorf, chair of the Commission on Wealth Creation and Social Cohesion, set up by Paddy Ashdown, wrote, 'My commission colleagues and I were not primarily concerned with inequality' (1995). In 1996, Victor Keegan, commenting on United Nations' figures which showed that the total wealth of the world's 358 billionaires equalled the combined incomes of the poorest 2.3 billion people, stated, 'These days it seems almost impolite, assuredly unfashionable – and even Old Labour – to dare to wonder if such outrageous maldistribution of wealth is fair. People just don't ask that sort of question at parties any more' (1996).

Even the Social Justice Commission, initiated by the Labour party, poured scorn on what it called 'the levellers' (1994). If anything, inequality has become a virtue. Conservative guru, Sir Keith Joseph declared in the election campaign of 1979, 'If we are to reduce poverty, we need more inequality not less.' His text was expounded again and again in the following years by politicians who claimed that only the prospect of extreme inequalities would make the able work hard for riches and the rest work hard to avoid destitution. And inequality was increased – as was poverty. The message has been continued by one of Sir Keith's successors in office, Peter Lilley who, in 1996, upheld inequality in Southwark Cathedral, saying, 'I searched my conscience in vain – with the possible exception of the parable of the vineyard – for suggestions that we must pursue equality and award equal incomes for equal effort, risk or skill.'

I want to put equality back on the public agenda. I believe that only a more equal society will reduce poverty. But more, I will argue that our Christian objective should go beyond the mere relief of poverty to the promotion of greater equality simply because this is in line with biblical thought. This can be shown by consideration of the creation, the Jubilee, the prophets, the incarnation, the life and teachings of Jesus, the cross and the example of the early Church.

The Bible and Equality

The Creation

The Bible records that 'God created human beings in his own image' (Genesis 1.27). If they are in his image then all humans must be of great value and, if all are created in the same way by God, they must also be of equal value to him. Richard Tawney concluded, 'The necessary corollary, therefore, of the Christian conception of man is a strong sense of equality. Equality does not mean that all men are equally clever or equally tall or equally fat. It means that all . . . are of equal value' (1981, pp. 182–3). A working party, set up by the Church of Scotland to study the Christian approach to the distribution of wealth, income and benefits, agreed that its starting point had to be the creation. It stated,

> The creation story, and in particular the affirmation that people are made in the image of God, is a strong statement that the original and proper situation is one of equality. Everyone is of the same infinite value in the eyes of God. There is in the created order no hierarchy or rankings, no inferiority or superiority, no dominance or subordination. The kind of fellowship which is God's original and final purpose for human beings, the condition for true human flourishing is that human beings should be treated as equally significant, equally important, equally entitled to love, equally capable of making a distinctive personal contribution to the enrichment of the community. (D. Forrester and D. Skene, eds, 1988, p. 67)

All people are equal before God. All people are created equal with each other. They were not made as different social classes or castes, as aristocrats or commoners, as superiors or inferiors. It follows that equality should be a foundation stone of God's society. It should be pursued in regard to relationships between human beings, in the distribution of opportunities and responsibilities, and in the allocation of resources. Professor Brian Griffiths wrote, 'Central to the Hebrew view of the material world is the belief that it is created by God and that it is intrinsically good. There is in creation an abundance and bounty, the promise of a land flowing with milk and honey. Poverty, famine and misery are not part of the Creator's intention for the world' (D. Anderson, ed., 1984, p. 108).

It follows that there are sufficient resources for all and – although I am not sure whether Professor Griffiths would go along with me on this – the implication is that they should be distributed in such a way as to avoid significant inequalities. Even after the biblical account of the fall and when God sent his creatures out to cultivate the land, there is no hint that the abundance of the earth was reserved for a minority. It was for the benefit of all. We are God's creation. The earth is the Lord's. The earth is for all his people.

The Jubilee

Over time, the sinfulness, the selfishness, the greed, the wrongful exploitation of the free choice which God gave to human beings, did lead to huge inequalities. Individuals acted as though wealth and power belonged to them, not God. They decided that if they could accumulate more and more through trade or war, then it was theirs to keep no matter how great the deprivations of others. The outcome was a divided society, rich and poor, the landed and the landless, free and slave, debt holders and debtors. Timothy Gorringe explains how the once egalitarian Israelite nation, partly due to its own sinfulness and foolishness in wanting a monarchy, became a grossly unequal nation. In response, the Lord God had a solution. Gorringe continues,

> The proposed answer to this problem was the Jubilee legislation. Every seven years (Deuteronomy) or every fifty years (Leviticus) debts must be remitted, and families returned to their patrimony. In this way class society would be periodically deconstructed. Redistributive justice ensured a return to equality of outcome. Justice in Israel was always conceived in terms of a passionate vindication of the poor and oppressed. (J. Boswell, ed., 1995, p. 13)

Interestingly, Brian Griffiths, well known as a defender of the private market economy, agrees that public or collective action was instituted in the Old Testament. After explaining that private ownership is approved within the Bible, he continues,

> It is also true, however, that constraints were built into the Mosaic law to put a sharp brake on the accumulation of property in a few hands. The Jubilee laws . . . were designed to prevent the development of a cycle of permanent deprivation.

And behind this principle of periodic restoration of an equable distribution of wealth was the idea that the people were the tenants of Yahweh. (D. Anderson, ed., p. 109)

These further points are worth adding about the Jubilee.

- It must be emphasized that the Jubilee legislation was a divine ordinance just as was the giving of the Ten Commandments. It was not meant to be optional. It laid down the ground rules for the economic and social life of the people. It was termed Jubilee because it meant rejoicing for those whose debts were abolished, for slaves who were freed, for the landless who received back their property as originally given.

- The Jubilee was built on the premise that land belonged to God. Human beings did not have rights to absolute ownership. It followed that collective action could be taken to redistribute it. In short, it is permissible for the community as a whole to reduce the 'ownership' of powerful individuals in order to create a better, more equal society which serves the interests of all.

- It was a sharing which did not exclude those who could be blamed for their losses – who are now called 'the undeserving poor' – and it was an act based upon the recognition that all things belong to a God who wants a society characterized by fairness, mercy, generosity and sharing, in short, not a divided society but a united one.

The Prophets

Sadly, the divine ordinances were largely ignored and so led to economic practices out of keeping with God's intentions. Consequently, one of the major themes of the prophets, those human messengers from God, was to condemn the powerful wealthy who, in promoting vast inequalities not only harmed their fellow creatures but also disobeyed God. Sometimes they focused on the behaviour of named individuals, including kings and high priests. More frequently, those such as Hosea, Amos, Micah and Isaiah, verbally lashed the whole Jewish nation for tolerating an economic system which allowed the greedy to exploit the weak, by paying low wages, by charging enormous interest rates on loans, and by taking their land. Isaiah raged,

'Woe betide those who enact unjust laws and draft repressive edicts, depriving the poor of justice, robbing the weakest of my people of their rights, plundering the widow and despoiling the fatherless!' (10.1–2).

Duncan Forrester and Danus Skene point out that at stake was not just individual charity with the affluent failing to give hand-outs to selected deserving cases. Rather the issue was 'restitution to the poor of what is properly theirs, restoration of God's just pattern of distribution' (p. 73). It was the whole economic and social system which had been corrupted. Inequality had replaced equality.

The last book of the Old Testament is that of Malachi. Like the other prophets he records God's anger against, 'sorcerers, adulterers, and perjurers, against those who cheat the hired labourer of his wages, who wrong the widow and the fatherless, who thrust the alien aside and do not fear me' (3.5). He pleads with the people to share with each other saying, 'Have we not all one father? Did not one God create us?' (2.10). He makes clear that this generosity should be applied not just to fellow Jews but to all, saying, 'The Lord's greatness reaches beyond the confines of Israel' (1.5). Malachi was expressing a growing message of Scripture that God's people have responsibilities not just to those who follow the Lord but to all. Then, somehow, Malachi perceived that God's love and justice were to be revealed in one who was to come, 'the sun of righteousness', the one who was to be the very embodiment of the Jubilee – Jesus.

The Incarnation

As a youngster, I was not sent to Sunday School or church. When, at last, I heard the gospel it came to me with a freshness which I found exciting. I was immensely attracted to the person of Jesus and amazed that God should enter the world in this human form. The incarnation is almost beyond belief and comprehension. It can be explained and understood only as the divine solution to the huge gap that had developed between God and his creation. It is how God finds a way to meet with, to be with, to explain him-self to and to reveal himself to his creatures. And his way was not to arrive in chariots of fire surrounded by blazing angels, not to suddenly appear before kneeling kings and emperors. Rather his way was to come in the form of a small infant, a baby dependent upon others, a child who was a member of an ordinary, probably poor, family. Of course, this is not to say that the Son of God was exactly the same as us. After all, he was the sinless one. It is to say that he came to be close to us. He was not identical with us but he did – and does – identify with us. And this is glorious. As the Scripture explains, 'So the Word became flesh; he made his home among us, and we saw his glory, such glory as befits the Father's only Son, full of grace and truth' (John 1.14).

Noticeably, God's chosen way – through his Son, Jesus – was not to distance himself from others by space, rank, status, possessions. Rather it was to be alongside them. It was the way of sharing the lifestyles, the difficulties, the joys, of his creation. It was the way which emphasized not inequality but equality. The mystery is that, in coming to earth, the Lord revealed both his divine lordship and his humanity. He made no secret that he was the Son of God and this was why the Jewish establishment determined to kill him – because 'he was claiming equality with God' (John 5.18). Yet Jesus did not use his position in order to dictate to others. Indeed, in regard to the way he lived, 'he laid no claim to equality with God, but made himself nothing, assuming the form of a slave' (Philippians 2.6–7). The mystery is that the one who is on a par with God lived in equality with humankind. In so doing, he laid down an example to be taken up by his followers who are not divine but who are the creatures of the divine. It is the example of attempting to enter into the lives of those in need, of being close to them, of identifying with them. It is the way of equality.

The Life and Teaching of Jesus

Jesus' life reflected the nature of his incarnation. For all of his childhood and most of his adulthood, he dwelt, played and toiled not in a palace but in a small village. Even when he toured the country proclaiming the gospel, he mixed not with the political, religious and commercial elites but mainly with those in everyday occupations – or no occupation. Jesus lived modestly, sharing the common purse with his friends. He was at ease with, was at one with, the men and women and children in the lower orders of a hierarchical society. Perhaps more remarkably still, he sought out the very poorest, the outcasts, the beggars, the blind, the lepers, the prostitutes, and befriended them, although in so doing he scandalized the religious leaders. He valued them all and, in so doing, demonstrated that all were equal in the sight of God. He thus set down a pattern of relating with others which Christians are called upon to emulate. Indeed, the same disciple John who wrote about his incarnation also wrote, 'whoever claims to be dwelling in him must live as Christ himself lived' (1 John 2.6).

The teaching of Jesus was as revolutionary as his practice. Even before he started his public ministry, his cousin John the Baptist prepared the way by telling those who waited for the Messiah, 'Whoever has two shirts must share with him who has none, and whoever has food must do the same' (Luke 3.10). Jesus then built upon this foundation by telling parables which praised the lowly and sincere rather than the powerful and the rich. The famous parable of the widow's mite taught that in God's eyes those with little who gave generously were more in accordance with his will than those who gave just a fraction of their riches. He commended mercy, compassion, sharing. He sent out his disciples with few possessions. And all the teaching and all the living was summed up, he said, in the two greatest commandments, namely, '"Love the Lord your God with all your heart, with all your soul, and with all your mind." That is the greatest, the first commandment. The second is like it: "Love your neighbour as yourself"' (Matthew 22.37-9). The two injunctions cannot be separated. Indeed Jesus also referred to them as one commandment. Human beings are intended to have a close, personal, loving, worshipping, relationship with God. Their God also created other human beings on a par with them and hence they must be loved as well. Further, we are to love them 'as ourselves'. If ever there was a divine pointer to the desirability of equality this is it. We are to treat our neighbours with the advantages we would give ourselves. Moreover, as Jesus revealed in his parables, the meaning of neighbours is not confined to our relatives, to the people next door, to the members of our ethnic group: it embraces all people. It even includes our enemies (Matthew 5.44). Again, the way we treat these neighbours is not confined to meeting their spiritual needs, it also embraces helping them materially, socially and emotionally. Surely, such a vision of neighbourliness must lead us to strive for a much more equal society in which others can have the same benefits as ourselves.

The incarnation, the lifestyle of Jesus and his teaching, are the divine intermingling with the human. They are not the stuff that can easily be expressed in academic and social scientific terms. But Jesus brought them together in the concept of servanthood. Amazingly, he described himself as a servant. Yet it was a description which angered the religious establishment because it involved the application of prophecy to himself. Jesus referred to the words of Isaiah, 'Here is my servant whom I have chosen, my beloved, in whom I take delight' (Matthew 12.18). The fact that Jesus was the servant was a confirmation that he was the Son of God. Further, the assumption of this role made clear just what his purpose was to be. The same verse continues, 'I will put my Spirit upon him, and he will proclaim justice among the nations.' Justice, that is, fairness linked with mercy, was the message while the medium was servanthood. In other words, the objective was to spread spiritual and social equality while the means of doing so was by being alongside the unequal.

That is not all. Jesus appointed disciples as the future leaders yet told them too to be servants. This servanthood implies leadership yet submission, instruction yet obedience, receiving yet giving. It is a mystery yet it is clear that all Christians are expected to be servants and that they should relate with others, not as authoritarian and distant directors, but rather as those who are strong in their beliefs and who convey them by sharing their lives with those in greatest need. This takes Christians into the framework of equality.

The Cross

The perfect life of Jesus and his supreme teaching led not to earthly honours, not to the first-century equivalent of an MBE or to the Jerusalem equivalent of a seat in the House of Lords. Instead, the outcome was an agonizing death nailed to a cross.

Central to our Christian faith is the belief that Christ's death was an act of atonement. He died that we might be forgiven. But there is more. George Carey, the Archbishop of Canterbury, wrote, 'We must reject as unbiblical any attempt to privatize the atonement, as if the only salvation that Christ had in mind was spiritual and other worldly'. The cross, he continued, also embodies the practice that we too must be prepared to make sacrifices for others as an expression of our love for and ties to them (1992, p. 179).

John Stott takes up this theme even more fully in his outstanding book *The Cross of Christ*. He rejoices that the meaning of the cross is about personal salvation but he expounds that it is also about the practice of sacrifice, service and suffering which Christians should apply to the home, the Church and the world. He regrets that the 'biblical vision of suffering service has been largely eclipsed in our day by the unbiblical "prosperity gospel" (which guarantees personal success) and by triumphalist notions of mission (which employ military metaphors that do not comfortably fit the image of the suffering servant)', instead of 'the renunciation of economic security and professional promotion, solidarity with the poor and needy'. He adds,

> Yet, as we have repeatedly noted throughout this book, the cross is a revelation of God's justice as well as of his love. That is why the community of the cross should concern itself with social justice as well as with loving philanthropy. It is never enough to have pity on the victims of injustice, if we do nothing to change the unjust situation itself . . . . If we love people, we shall be concerned to secure their basic rights as human beings, which is also the concern of justice. The community of the cross which has truly absorbed the message of the cross, will always be motivated to action by the demands of justice and love. (1986, pp. 291–3)

What is the injustice to be countered? What are those basic rights of human beings? They must be related to the fact that all human beings are equal before God. As we kneel before the cross, we are before the one who died for *all*. Moreover, we kneel together for we are all kin and we have no differences of status or deservability before him – equality. Given this oneness, it is unacceptable, it is a denial of basic rights, that some of our kin are deprived of decent incomes, homes, health, education, opportunities, careers, while others have them to excess – inequality. The cross is often said to be the place where love and justice meet. Its teaching is that our love for our kin should make us prepared to make individual sacrifices so that they have the same material, social and spiritual blessings as ourselves. Its teaching is also that God requires justice so we should be ready to promote community and political action to bring in new societal structures which are rooted in equality.

The New Testament Church

The practices of the Spirit-filled early church members are well known. 'All the believers agreed to hold everything in common: they began to sell their property and possessions and distribute to everyone according to his need' (Acts 2.44–5). Later the Church was involved in putting aside certain members to help those in need (Acts 6.1–7). The history of the Church, as recorded in the book of Acts, is a vivid testimony that Christianity is about sharing, is about action to meet material needs, and that the pursuit of material justice goes hand in hand with spiritual outpourings.

However, Acts is often regarded as a record apart from the epistles which follow it in the New Testament. The implication is that the great Paul distanced himself from social and material matters. Of course, this ignores completely the letter of James with its ringing condemnation of the rich who oppress the poor and the insistence that faith and practical action must go together. But it is also wrong in regard to the teaching of Paul. It is clear that he did not exhort the young churches to withdraw into insular and cosy groups to spend their time discussing the minutiae of theology, with the greatest plaudits going to those who achieved the equivalent of a PH D in Religious Studies. Instead he exhorted them to be a model of relationships and behaviour for the rest of society. In his commentary on Ephesians, which he subtitles 'God's New Society', the evangelical scholar, John Stott, draws attention to a central message and practice of the new Church, namely that it broke down all barriers between Jew and Gentile, male and female, slave and free so that 'inequality before God is abolished' (1994, p. 259). It will be retorted that this means just spiritual equality and, after all, that Paul upheld earthly slavery. Not so. If a slave owner accepted that all were equal before God then the onus was upon him 'to develop a relationship in which he gave them the *same* [Stott's emphasis] treatment as he hoped to receive' (p. 259). He concludes, 'A message which thus united master and slave as brothers *ipso facto* issued its radical challenge to an institution which separated them as proprietor and slave. Thereafter it was only a matter of time. "Slavery would be abolished from within"' (p. 259). Drawing upon the basic belief that all are equal before God, Christians applied it practically within their own churches, then within their own communities and then – as Stott explains – to society at large.

It is not my intention to claim that equality is the only, or even the major, theme of the Bible. It is certainly not my wish to deflect attention away from the Christian message that individuals need to meet with, to find forgiveness with, and to come into a personal relationship with God. I write as one who became a Christian by conversion. But, in doing so, my understanding of the Scriptures is that, as all are equal before God, so all have an equal claim to the privileges and responsibilities of God's world. Equality certainly is one of the significant messages of the Bible. Richard Tawney, surely the greatest Christian scholar on the theme of equality, takes up the text, as given in the Authorized Version from Mary's inspired message before the birth of Jesus, 'He hath put down the mighty from their seats and exalted them of lowly degree' (Luke 1.52). He comments,

> Pondering that and other indiscretions of a neglected classic, I find it impossible to believe, with some Christians, that the love of God, whom one has not seen, is compatible with the advantages snatched from the brother whom one sees every day, or that what they describe as spiritual equality, a condition which they neither created nor – happily – can alter, has its appropriate corollary economic, social and educational inequalities which, given the will, they can abolish out of hand .... A Christianity which resigns the economic world to the devil appears to me, in short, not Christianity at all. (1981, pp. 164–5)

This is God's world and I believe that we, God's creatures, have a responsibility to shape it, to order it, to preserve it, in keeping with the principles which he has revealed. Spiritually, socially, economically, we should strive for a more equal society.

2

～◦◦～

The Unequal Society

It is not denied that social conditions in general have improved in Britain during the present century, an improvement which owes much to the creation of the welfare state. My grandfather, a bricklayer in Barking, recorded in his memoirs that he was made unemployed in 1904. He wrote, 'There being no unemployment insurance at that time, the five pounds we had saved was soon expended.' The family was saved from the workhouse because their landlady allowed them to stay rent free in their rooms until grandfather eventually got a job on the railways. Even so, when in 1914 he was knocked over by a train, there was no sickness benefit while he was absent from work for several weeks. For people like him, and his successors, poverty was alleviated by the introduction of state unemployment pay and, later, by the establishment of the National Health Service.

Conditions have improved. But not all sections of the population have benefited to the same degree from rising standards of living. As Frank Field explained back in 1974, 'It is as if the poor have been placed on an escalator ... but the rich, too, are on board their own escalator which is moving just as fast if not faster. The existence of the cycle of inequality is well known to the poor' (1974, p. 62). Since Frank Field wrote, the second escalator has quickened its pace so that today inequalities are even more marked, as will now be shown.

Income

The Growing Gap

In the previous chapter, it was made clear that poverty was extensive and growing. Yet, simultaneously, the number of affluent

16

people has also increased, with the result of a growing gap between the incomes of different sections of the population. In her comprehensive review of public expenditure and fiscal policies, Sally Holtermann stated,

> During the 1980s, the real incomes of the better-off rose significantly while those of the least well-off actually fell. The median person in the richest tenth of the population saw real income (before housing costs) increase by 58% between 1979 and 1990/91 compared with a 1% decline for the middle person in the poorest tenth . . . the share of total national income received by people in the bottom 20% of the income distribution fell from 9.6% to 6.2%, while the share received by the top 50% rose from 68% to 75%. (1995, p. 42)

Indeed, the gap between the highest and the lowest paid is now greater than at any time since records began in 1880.

The Joseph Rowntree Foundation set up an inquiry into income and wealth. Composed of a cross-section of political figures, industrialists and trade unionists and chaired by Sir Peter Barclay, its findings were published in 1995 as *The Inquiry Into Income and Wealth*. Its major conclusion was that inequality was widespread in Britain and that income inequality had grown faster in Britain since 1977 than in any other comparable industrial society. It made clear that economic growth had occurred, but that the poorest 20 to 30 per cent had failed to share in it.

The Institute for Fiscal Studies calculated that for the period 1985–95, the top 10 per cent of households were on average £1,627.60 a year better off, while the bottom 10 per cent were £156 a year worse off (cited by H. Russell, 1995, p. 58).

In 1996, the United Nations published a worldwide study entitled *Human Development Report*. Victor Keegan explained how inequality was measured and drew out its findings for the United Kingdom,

> Economists measure inequality by the so-called Gini coefficient where zero is perfect equality and 100 is complete inequality. Normally movements in inequality happen so slowly that they are hard to detect. But Anthony Atkinson, Warden of Nuffield College, a leading expert in this area, reckons that between 1977 and 1991 the coefficient for the UK rose by a very sharp 10 percentage points (much more than in other countries). (V. Keegan, 1996)

This is not to say that no movement occurs between different
income levels. Some in the lowest 10 per cent of income recipients
do – sometimes temporarily – move up; but others move down.
Society is not static. None the less, huge differences in income
remain.

Explanations

Clearly, the rich have become richer, the poor have become
poorer. Why? The following explanations contribute to the
answer.

- Unemployment and economic inactivity has risen steeply
  with those officially counted as out of work rising from 1.4
  million to 3 million during 1979–91. The result has left
  many more people dependent upon state benefits at a time
  when salaries for some employed workers were rising. Over
  the last fifteen years, the value of Income Support for a
  married couple as a proportion of average, full-time, male
  earnings has dropped from 26 per cent to 19 per cent.
- The difference between workers and unemployed was
  magnified by a growth both in households which had two
  earners and also in those which had none. The Rowntree
  Report explained that between 1975 and 1993 the number of
  'work rich' households grew from 51 to 61 per cent while
  those of 'work poor' households went up from 3 to 11 per cent.
- Amongst the employed, the abolition of government
  machinery, which protected wage levels in some industries,
  has stimulated the development of a low-wage sector.
  Between 1986 and 1995, the wages of the lowest paid, full-
  time male workers fell from 0.69 to 0.64 of the average wage.
  The Rowntree Report expressed particular concern about
  the wage plight of ethnic minorities and young people.
  Whereas 18 per cent of the white population was in the
  poorest fifth of the population, more than a third of non-
  whites were in this position. Concerning young people, of
  those born after 1960, there was a bottom 10 per cent whose
  real wages were well below those of their predecessors.
- Government tax changes have tended to favour the affluent
  at the expense of the poor. There has been a shift towards
  indirect taxation, such as VAT. As such taxes are levied without regard to income, they hit the poorest most hard.

Within income tax, tax cuts have benefited those with high incomes so that 45 per cent of all cuts since 1979 have gone to the top 10 per cent of income recipients. Simultaneously, the level of income at which families pay tax has fallen so more low earners have been drawn into the tax system.

Wealth

Wealth is even more unequally distributed than income with its ownership long-concentrated in the hands of a small minority. None the less, from the 1930s to the 1970s the proportion owned by the top 10 per cent of the population did drop slightly to 50 per cent of all wealth. However, Professor Meghnad Desai points out, 'This trend was reversed during the years when Baroness Thatcher was prime minister and by 1989 the figure had increased again to 53 per cent' (1996). Between 1986 and 1992, that owned by the least wealthy 50 per cent of the population fell from 10 per cent to 8 per cent.

A distinction is usually made between 'production wealth', that is, land, shares, government securities, ownership of firms, etc. and 'domestic wealth' such as houses, vehicles, household goods. The former is particularly concentrated in a minority of hands which gives them enormous economic power in our society. The latter, along with shares in former public utilities, has become more widely distributed: in 1979 just over half the adult population owned their own homes; by 1992 it was two-thirds. However, this still leaves behind a substantial minority. Thus Carol Oppenheim and Lisa Harker write of 'The third of society who are excluded from owning a home are forced to rely on a shrinking and impoverished public and privately rented sector' (1996, p. 176). These citizens – unemployed, long-term sick and disabled people and non-working lone parents – are frequently contained within inner city zones and run-down estates, sometimes referred to as ghettos. Lacking both kinds of wealth, they have become increasingly distanced from other members of society.

Employment Conditions

Clearly, the top sectors of the population enjoy not just high pay but also secure employment, many perks, company cars, paid holidays, golden handshakes if they leave, and high-level pensions when they retire. For many, employment conditions have improved vastly. For instance, in 1996 a new quango, the North of Scotland Water Authority, on taking over responsibility from local authorities, promptly presented its chief managers with cars worth £20,000 as part of an improved employment package. Top directors in local authorities also earn in excess of £50,000 a year, have generous car and travel allowances, good holidays, and high pensions. Ironically, some of them supervise services for some of the poorest people in society. The growth of quangos has provided the favoured elites with even more opportunities for high rewards for minimal time. The chairman of the Port of London Authority gets £50,000 a year for a time commitment of twelve days a year, the chairman of the London Docklands Development Corporation £25,000 for two days a week, and members of the Broadcasting Standards Council around £12,845 for spending about two days a week watching TV and listening to radio programmes which are subject to complaints. Nice little earners for those who already have extensive incomes from other jobs and other sources.

By contrast, the work conditions of those at the bottom of the equality–inequality line have deteriorated. As the government has abolished low wage protection, so wages have dropped and hours increased. A parliamentary answer given on 1 February 1996, revealed that research on Job Centre vacancies showed that 11 per cent of vacancies were for hourly rates of pay of £2.50 or below and 47 per cent for £2.51–£3.50. In all, six out of every ten job vacancies produced a weekly income of around £140 for a forty-hour week. However, more and more people are not in full-time jobs. Between 1981 and 1992, the proportion of economically active people working part-time grew from 19 per cent to 24 per cent of the labour force. During 1994–5, of all the people placed in posts by the Employment Service, only 48 per cent went into full-time, permanent posts. There was an expansion in part-time jobs, temporary posts, jobs which people had to leave on taking their holidays, jobs without pensions.

The lone mother of a boy, who attended the youth clubs with which I am associated, had worked for a number of years as a cleaner with a public service. When the service was privatized, she was offered less work, less pay, less holidays – take it or leave it. She had to take it.

The head of a quango, the cleaner in an office, they are both the creation of God. Yet employment practice is treating them like two different species and the inequalities in employment are widening.

Housing

Although housing conditions have improved vastly during this century, a substantial number of citizens have been on a very slow escalator of improvement. Indeed, in recent years their escalator has gone into reverse. The number of families enjoying luxury homes with spare bedrooms, double glazing, double garages and large gardens has increased. Yet in this same Britain, in 1991, some 6 per cent of households were overcrowded, that is were living at densities of one or more persons per room. It is worth noting that overcrowding is particularly found amongst lone parent families, 8.2 per cent, and those of Asian origin, 24.8 per cent. Affluent families now take central heating and dry walls for granted. Yet 20 per cent of all dwellings in England and over 25 per cent in Scotland in 1991 were damp. Increasing numbers now own or have access to two homes. By contrast, others have none. In 1986, the number of households accepted by local authorities in Britain as homeless and who were found some kind of accommodation was 118,000. By 1992 it was 167,000 – and these figures do not include most homeless single people. In 1986 in England 20,800 families were in temporary accommodation. By 1992 it was 62,900. Many of these were living in bed and breakfast hostels.

Glossy magazines show photographs of the wealthy in their glitzy homes displaying furniture which costs more than some families earn in a year, and overlooking lawns the size of a football pitch. I visited a family in bed and breakfast accommodation in Glasgow. Descending the stairs, I saw a notice pinned on the wall, 'No children upstairs, no playing on the stairs'. The family of two adults and three children were in one basement room. There were insufficient chairs. It was cold. A child sat on one of the two beds staring at – but not really watching – a flickering black and white television. There was no access to a garden. The mother, in order to relieve the tension between the family members, often spent time outside walking the streets with the children.

Again, I am looking at a section of a Sunday newspaper headed 'Money Matters'. It reports that two of Bath's finest town houses are on the market at £300,000 each. Of course, readers might want one as a second home in order to escape from London for the weekend.

Not far from me, a neighbour showed me her sons' bedroom. It contained two beds, no cupboards, no heating. A huge damp patch on wall and ceiling. Downstairs, fungus grew in the toilet. She is desperate to move. She followed up advertisements for private flats on the other side of town and was rebuffed by the demands for £250 key money. We approached a charity which was prepared to help with this: she sought another flat – dry, furnished, roomy, even a small garden – but the rent was above the maximum amount she could get from Housing Benefit. No chance of escape. Inequality in housing.

Opportunities

A few months ago, I collected some teenagers from a holiday. The adventure holiday was great value at £100 per child, yet our local project had had to apply to a charity to subsidize the young-sters. They had a great time, learning to ride horses, canoeing, making new friendships with young people from other parts of the country and relating well with the staff of Teen Ranch, the Christian agency which organizes the activity. As our minibus entered Easterhouse, a seventeen-year-old spoke up, 'Wish I could have stayed there. Wish I could work there. Look at this place.' He is unemployed. 'This place' is his dingy street. A fifteen-year-old joined in, 'I wish I could get out.' His father is long-term unem-ployed and the chances of getting out are small. Both these teenagers have some talent in sport but even developing this has depended on charitable grants. Their intellectual and sporting hopes are unlikely to be fulfilled for they are in an environment where opportunities are limited.

The same week, a TV documentary focused on Gordonstoun School where the children of the privileged received an education and training which gave them access to sports coaching and then a route to secure, well-paid jobs. They could achieve, study, travel. Yet their basic abilities, I considered, were no better than my two young friends. But the privileged received more privileges, the deprived more deprivations. Inequality of opportunity.

Power

The final inequality to be mentioned in this section, perhaps the one that controls all others, is the inequality of power. Those at the bottom of the pile are comparatively powerless. Of course, they may have degrees of power or influence within their families or amongst their friends, but they have few if any means of improving their material conditions or ways of life to any marked degree. Power implies choice and David Vincent in his historical examination of poverty explains that, in the period 1900–1914, the powerlessness of the poor was revealed in the limited nature of choice amongst poor people. They could rarely choose to get off the bottom layer of society and their choices were restricted to deciding which basic goal of life should be lost in order to gain another basic goal. Thus 'If a particular member of a family was adequately fed, the others were not; if the fire was burning well, the table was ill-provided; if cultural hunger was diminished, bodily nutrition was increased; if short-term respite was supplied by a money lender, long-term recovery was postponed; if recourse to the poor law prevented physical extinction, nevertheless it destroyed social standing' (1991, pp. 3–4). Today standards may have risen but for many choices are still restricted: if money is spent on a new pair of shoes for one child then money is not available for another to go on a school trip: if savings are made for one child to go on a holiday with the youth club, then a much needed new fire cannot be purchased. In the short term, money can be borrowed from a loan shark to get the washing machine repaired but, in the long term, it will be difficult to get out of his grip. Perhaps most obviously, those at the lower end of society cannot choose where to live. Place of residence often determines which schools are on offer to local families, the number of GPs available, the number of dentists, the variety of shops, the amount of green space and so on. The affluent can usually choose to live in a favoured area, the deprived cannot. The former thus have more power over their lifestyles.

But the differences in power go beyond this. Residents of council estates, dwellers in the deprived inner cities, those dependent on welfare benefits have little power in regard to the way they are treated by social institutions. They do not make the rules, they do not determine the policies. They tend not to be local government councillors, let alone MPs. In contrast, are those who

possess the incomes, the assets, the contacts with the establishment, the positions within political parties, which allow them to
choose and change, to shape society into their mould. The
inequalities of power.

At the top of society are those who hold political, financial and
media power, who are in government, who control capital, who
head major institutions, who are in the professions, who shape
the content of the mass media. A Christian view is that they
should use their political, economic and social power to promote
the common good, to spread privileges and resources, to reduce
injustices, to uphold integrity and honesty. In short, the Christian concept of service is that they should use their power and
influence not for themselves but for others. Leaders have rarely
acted in such altruistic ways but there is little doubt that during
the 1980s and 1990s our society has reached a position where the
mighty have allowed selfishness to rule, where they have been
obsessed with promoting their own material wealth and status. In
short, the inequalities of power are exploited in order to magnify
inequalities of other kinds.

It is seen in politics. The Nolan Committee strongly criticized
the behaviour of MPs who regarded their position as a means of
making money outside of their parliamentary salaries. A few
months after the publication of the Nolan Report, government
ministers quietly inserted into the Finance Bill of 1996 a number
of financial clauses to their own benefit: one exempted them –
unlike other taxpayers – from paying income tax on their chauffeur driven cars which took them to work; a second allowed the
Deputy Prime Minister to be paid £40,000 a year tax-free in
order to use his own car and chauffeur on public business; a third
enabled spouses to gain from publicly paid travel, meals and
accommodation when accompanying ministers abroad and elsewhere. All this at the very time when government was passing
legislation which made life harder for poor people.

The Christian MP, David Alton, after years in the House of
Commons, wrote powerfully,

> The motivation behind our sleazy state is as old as the hills; the
> pursuit of power, personal aggrandizement and the protection
> of privilege. We have passed through a decade when we were
> all encouraged to consume and acquire. The 'me first' society
> in which everything has a price and nothing a value promoted
> as good business practice, unbridled individualism, personal

greed and rapacious competitiveness. As government has adopted business practice at the expense of service, so the values of the financial jungle have become the civic values of our own time. The real tragedy is that most politicians do not regard such a morality as corrupt. Some will even defend it as sound market practice. Meanwhile, the public has come to expect nothing better from the system. (1994)

As Alton implies, many politicians use power to promote their own interests and, in so doing, encourage others in society to do likewise. In short, they escalate inequalities.

This inequality of power is also seen in private enterprise with boardroom power used for individual advancement regardless of the adverse effects on others. A company wins a franchise for a railway service and immediately axes thousands of staff, reduces the number of trains and provides directors and shareholders with vast financial gains. In March 1996, the remuneration of the chief executive of Barclays Bank was raised to £791,000 a year. In the same week, the bank announced 1,000 job cuts. Power is thus used to provide the rich with yet more material affluence at the cost of redundancy and unemployment – with all its associated sufferings for the families concerned – for those without power.

It is seen in the mass media. Clearly much power rests with those who have access to the major means of communication. In theory, those in control could ensure that the disadvantaged have a voice. Instead the reverse has happened. Consider *Question Time*, the BBC's main forum of public debate. In the 1980s, I published an analysis of its panels' membership and repeated this in 1990 (1994). Participants are overwhelmingly made up of politicians, journalists, heads of financial and business organizations and the top brass from quangos. Whatever their precise occupation, their characteristics are similar – very affluent, powerful, mainly drawn from the southern establishment and likely to be listed in *Who's Who*. The same kind of people, indeed often the very same people, also appear on radio's *Any Questions*. Especially interesting is TV's *Newsnight* often headed by Jeremy Paxman. Paxman wrote a popular book entitled *Friends in High Places: who rules Britain?* in which he criticized inequality in Britain and in particular condemned the fact that top positions in society were still biased towards the products of public schools and Oxbridge (1991). Yet on this programme, he tends to interview people from just those backgrounds. The programmes often discuss such matters as unemployment, the economy, crime, social security, wages, housing, etc. Of course, the participants do have views worth listening to. But completely excluded from the panels are low-wage earners, the unemployed, residents of the inner cities and council estates. Excluded are the very people who do know what it is like to wait for hours to cash a giro at the Post Office, to despair of countless job rejections, to have a child sick in a damp-ridden home, to be unable to afford an electricity power card. It is true that programmes might sometimes include such people in audiences who might be allowed to contribute a quick sentence before being cut off. But they are not allowed to develop their analysis, their views on policy, in the way that the privileged are encouraged to do. The assumption is that they are not worthy to be on the panels or are not articulate enough.

In 1996, Channel 4 made the brave decision to broadcast a season of programmes about poverty under the title 'Broke'. A trio of features examined the shaky foundations of the British economy and explained how the dominance of the free market had multiplied unemployment and poverty. Other documentaries and films depicted the plight of drug abusers, of abandoned children, of those in the hands of illegal loan sharks. The problems were well conveyed. Yet the presenters of the programmes were always the affluent. Poor people were kept out of the positions of power. They were not allowed to debate. Their views were not considered worthy of respect. In short, even in programmes about poverty, the media functions to uphold inequalities of power.

The same exclusion applies in the press. *The Guardian*, more than most papers, is sympathetic to poor people. Yet, when it published an eight-page supplement on the 1993 budget, there were comments from sixty-two contributors, from well-paid journalists, from Oxbridge economists, from seven wise and wealthy women and seven wise and powerful men. Yet not one sentence was written by poor people or their representatives, although their lives were markedly affected by the budget.

The media is thus another expression of inequality. People at the bottom end of society are regarded as specimens to be discussed, not as human beings who can discuss. Their intelligence and abilities are written off. In short, they are not regarded as equal with other members of society. Thus power in the media is exploited to ensure that the views and interests of the privileged are conveyed while those of the deprived are neglected.

Again, this inequality of power is seen not just in the media but in other expressions of public feeling towards poor people. Government ministers sometimes sneer at poverty-stricken lone mothers yet are respectful towards royal lone parents. The Minister of Social Security, Peter Lilley, has castigated Income Support recipients who abuse the system and has launched an expensive campaign to catch them. Of course, such fraud should be stopped. But, simultaneously, the government shows little concern about tax evasion – estimated at up to £6.3 billion a year – and actually cuts the number of Inland Revenue staff. The message is that the crimes of the poor are dreadful and to be pursued while those of the affluent are just a game to be taken lightly. The inequality is that those at the bottom have few means of challenging the attitudes and hypocrisies of those at the top.

Enough has been written to demonstrate that Britain is riven with inequalities. Whether it is regarding income, wealth, employment conditions, housing, lifestyles, power or access to the media, ours is a society which is deeply riven by the social divisions of inequality. In his best selling book, *The State We're In*, Will Hutton argues persuasively that Britain is a 40/30/30 society. At the top are the 40 per cent who enjoy high salaries and secure employment, who dwell in affluent homes in green suburbs, who possess every comfort along with regular holidays and who are increasingly drawing upon private systems of education, health and pensions that mark them out as superior to other citizens. In the middle are the 30 per cent who thought they were safe with moderate incomes, semi-detached houses and vacations in Spain but who now find that changes in work practices are making their jobs insecure, who are becoming 'insecurely self-employed, involuntarily part-time, or casual workers' so that they now need two earners to ensure that the mortgage can always be paid. At the bottom are the 30 per cent which Hutton calls the marginalized: they include the unemployed, those who are in and out of work and the very low paid; they are frequently dependent upon public services which are deteriorating under cash shortages; they tend to live in the least desirable areas of the big cities where they, more than others, are the victims of crime and environmental pollution; their children are the ones least likely to succeed at school and to find worthwhile jobs (1995, p. 14). Hutton writes with broad strokes and details can be questioned. The exact percentages may be open to correction. The three groups are not quite so physically separated as he indicates. But the core rings true. Britain is an unequal society. Britain is an increasingly unequal society. The structure of British society is at odds with a Christian understanding both of how all human beings should be regarded and also of how they should be treated.

3

⚬⟞

So What?

Britain is characterized by extensive poverty and wide inequalities. So what? Aren't the poor supposed to be happy? Sometimes, after addressing meetings which contain members who have reached positions of importance from humble beginnings, I get the response. 'We didn't have anything. Not like the spongers today who get everything they ask for – even holidays abroad. We had nothing when we were children but we all looked after each other, we were poor but happy.' Looking at their mournful faces and listening to their grumpy tones, I wonder just why they struggled so hard to leave their former happy states. Certainly, today as well as yesterday, those on low incomes do help each other, do make sacrifices for their children, do often display a cheerfulness in adversity. But, in general, poverty does not make for happiness. My grandfather's poverty brought him fear and worry.

Today I live in an area where poverty and unemployment have increased in the last two decades. Obviously the increase is accompanied by anything but happiness. Adults are depressed at being out of work, crime rises, and more unemployed youngsters turn to drug abuse. These may be extreme and glaring examples but those citizens at the bottom of an unequal society – I will sometimes refer to them as poor people for short – are also liable to other factors which make for human suffering. For poverty is associated with a number of physical and social disadvantages not borne equally by other members of society.

The Disadvantages of Inequality

Ill-Health

A government agency, the Health Educational Council, concluded from an extensive review of the research, 'However poverty or social disadvantage is measured, the link with ill-health is clear and consistent' (M. Whitehead, ed., 1987, p. 19). Poor people are much more likely than other sections of the population to suffer ill-health. They are more liable to cardiovascular diseases, gastro-intestinal diseases, chronic respiratory diseases and infections and accidents. Sometimes the greater ill-health of low-income groups is blamed on themselves with particular attention drawn to the fact that they are more likely to smoke. There is evidence that poor people tend to smoke to relieve both tension and bore-dom but it cannot be disputed that it does contribute to certain illnesses. However, it is also true, as Sally Holtermann explains, that the association with poverty holds good even when factors such as smoking are taken into account (1995, p. 119). Overall, the life expectancy of people in Social Class V is seven years lower than that in Social Class I.

The connection applies as much to children as to adults. Children from Social Class V are much more likely than other children to suffer from low birth weight, long-standing illnesses, from pneumonia, and from respiratory diseases including chronic coughs and asthma. They are also likely to be thinner and lighter. The vulnerability of poor children was graphically presented in a study of low-income families known to Family Service Units. Seventy per cent reported ill-health or disability among their children. Asthma, bronchitis and eczema were common. Kidney disease, depression, growth problems and behavioural difficulties were also frequently reported (R. Cohen, et al., 1992). In 1996, the Health Visitors' Association reported the re-emergence of tuberculosis and rickets amongst poor children.

Children from poor backgrounds are also much more vulner-able to accidents. The children of Social Class V parents are six times more likely to die from burns than those from Social Class I. Child deaths from head injuries are sixteen times higher in deprived areas. Children from low income homes, that is, those which generally do not own cars, are – ironically – particularly vulnerable to traffic accidents. In 1988 in Easterhouse, the pro-portion of children injured so seriously that they were kept in hospital was nearly double that of Glasgow as a whole. It must be said that since 1981 child accident deaths have fallen in Britain. But the drop is most marked amongst the affluent with little improvement amongst the least well-off. Thus between 1979–83 the injury death rate for children in Social Class V was 3.5 times higher than for Social Class I. By 1989–92, the difference had grown to five times. It is the children of the poor whose bodies are at greatest risk of being burnt, broken, even destroyed.

Thankfully, during this century there has been a significant decline in infant mortality. However, the gap between different social groupings remains. In regard to perinatal mortality – children stillborn or dying in their first week – in 1992, nine out of every 1,000 babies born into Social Class V died compared with six in Social Class I. In regard to infant mortality, deaths in the first year of life, eight out of every 1,000 died in Social Class V compared with five from Social Class I. The gap between the social classes is not being reduced, indeed the most recent indications are that it is broadening.

These figures are for the nation as a whole. The huge disadvantages of poor families becomes more obvious when local figures are used. Michael Pacione explains that, within Glasgow, health inequality 'is starkly demonstrated by comparison of figures for deaths in the first year of life between Easterhouse (with a rate of 46.7 per 1,000) and the nearby middle-class suburb of Bishopbriggs (10.0 per 1,000)' (1995, p. 225). Even before birth, the perinatal mortality rate in Easterhouse families is over three times as high as that in professional families. But figures alone do not convey the feelings of those whose children die. In our neighbourhood, a lone mother was devastated when her eleven-year-old son, whom she had raised so well, was run over and killed by a bus. A young mother asked our Salvation Army officer to bury her thirteen-day-old baby. This is not unusual, for the nearby Church of Scotland minister reports that he has buried more children in his few years in Easterhouse than other ministers will in their whole ministries. Poverty and the death of young children are close neighbours.

The above indications that people in poverty are at a health disadvantage compared with other citizens is not new. A more recent finding is the link between unemployment and ill-health. The immediate trauma of redundancy and the effects of long-term unemployment are associated not just with psychological symptoms such as depression, but also with physical ones such as raised cholesterol and blood pressure. Tragically, unemployment also kills. A link between being out of work and suicide has long been known. But longitudinal studies of mortality now also show a more general link with premature death. As Dr Richard Smith concluded in *The British Medical Journal*, 'The evidence that unemployment kills – particularly the middle-aged – now verges on the irrefutable' (1991).

Educational Underachievement

Educational achievement is vitally important in our society both as a means of self-fulfilment and also as a means of obtaining employment. A further disadvantage suffered by children from the poorer families, that is, those at the bottom end of inequality, is that they tend to achieve less at both primary and secondary schools than those from more affluent backgrounds. These differences hold good even when abilities are taken into account. Recent research in Northern Ireland shows that in primary schools, where no more than 10 per cent of pupils are in receipt of free meals, 52 per cent gained a grade A in tests for selective schools; in those where over half were entitled to free meals, only 16 per cent obtained this grade. Not surprisingly, in Britain in 1990–1, only 3 per cent of young people from poor backgrounds went on to obtain degrees compared with 32 per cent of the affluent.

The association between social deprivations and educational underachievement can also be found between different types of areas. Sally Holtermann states that 'In many deprived urban areas in England, the proportion of 15 year olds leaving school with no graded qualifications is higher than the average for all England' (p. 110). In Scotland, a comparison can be made between a secondary school in Easterhouse in the eastern and poorer side of Glasgow with a well-known high school on the western and affluent side. In the former school, in 1992, only 1 per cent of its fourth years gained three or more Standard grades at levels 1–2; in the latter it was 30 per cent. The following year, the percentage leaving to go on to full-time higher education in the former school was too low to be recorded; in the latter it was 36 per cent.

There is little doubt that having low-income parents or coming from deprived areas can have an adverse effect on education; and some children come from both poor parents and poor areas. The outcomes are well brought out in research compiled by the Glasgow Health Board for the year 1988. It shows that children coming from both an advantaged home and an advantaged area have a 70 per cent chance of attaining three or more SCE Highers;

those from an advantaged home and disadvantaged area 26 per cent; those from a disadvantaged home and an advantaged area 22 per cent; and those from a disadvantaged home and a disadvantaged area 3 per cent (Glasgow Director of Public Health, 1993). Poverty whether of home or area or both does constitute a serious educational handicap.

It must be emphasized that sometimes children with the most severe social disadvantages do succeed in education and employment. The treasurer of the local project with which I am associated in Easterhouse was born in and went to school in the area and he is now a deputy headmaster. Yet these individuals are the exceptions and do not compensate for the many who miss out. The disadvantage is twofold. Their abilities may not be developed to the same extent as pupils from more favoured backgrounds. Further, even if they overcome this handicap and achieve educational qualifications at school, they may not move on to higher education which is now the gateway to employment.

Removal Into Public Care

Perhaps the most tragic disadvantage suffered by children from homes characterized by social deprivations is their greater vulnerability to being removed into public care. Children can be admitted or committed to the care of local authorities through a number of administrative and legal routes. Yet, whatever the channel, they frequently have one factor in common – poverty. In the 1970s, a six-year study in Newcastle found that over 80 per cent of children taken into the local authority's care were from low-income families (L. Rhodes and J. Veit Wilson, 1978). In 1984–5, Saul Becker and Stuart MacPherson discovered that in Strathclyde Region, 88 per cent of all referrals for child care matters came from low-income families (1986). The most recent research, by Matthew Colton and his colleagues in Wales, found that 72 per cent of the child care cases of the Social Services Departments concerned the children of unemployed parents (1997).

This is not to say that all socially deprived children do enter care for, in fact, most poor parents do cope with and retain the care of their children. It is to say that families at the bottom end of the inequality line are much more vulnerable than other parents to the risk of being separated from their children. Andrew

Bebbington and John Miles, in their study of 2,500 children in public care, noted that over three-quarters of their parents received Income Support while over half lived in socially deprived areas. They compiled a probability chart which demonstrated that 'A child whose family is not on income support, is in a two-parent family with three or fewer children, is white, and lives in a spacious, owner occupied house, has only a 1 in 7,000 chance of entering care. A child from a large, one-parent family, living on income support, of mixed ethnic origin, and dwelling in a crowded, privately rented home, has a 1 in 10 chance' (1989). Children accommodated in public care are predominantly the children of the poor.

Why?

Clearly, an unequal society submits those at the bottom end to circumstances, conditions and experiences which are associated with much greater ill-health, educational failure, family separations and other disadvantages than are faced by other sections of the population. Such outcomes should be greatly disturbing to Christians. They conflict with Christian belief that the good things of the earth should be distributed fairly. They contradict Christian understanding that God values all people and that this value has to be expressed in the ways in which they are treated by their fellow human beings. They raise the issue of sin. If God's intention was that his resources should be used fairly for the well-being of all his creatures, then it is sinful if, for instance, the government pays the Health Service and Parliamentary Ombudsman £104,431 a year yet allows some families to receive only £9,000 a year. It is a manifestation of evil if, in Scotland, the businessman Mr Bruno Schroder possesses wealth amounting to £860 million which is more than the assets of whole council schemes where hundreds of children live physically stunted and socially restricted lives. Such unequal distributions do not occur by accident. They occur because human beings allow their society to be so ordered that they can occur. These orderings are sinful because, as the Bible says, 'to oppress the poor is to insult the Creator' (Proverbs 14.31). If Christians take seriously their responsibility to oppose sin and evil – or whatever it is called – then they have an obligation to attempt to counter these gross inequalities.

The findings also lead to the question 'why?' I am not asking the fundamental question why do inequalities arise in the first place. Professors Vic George and Irving Howards, after a review of genetical, pathological, cultural, Marxist and other class explanations, can only conclude that 'Advanced industrial societies are stratified along class, gender and race lines so that economic and political power is unequally distributed' (1991, p. 93). At least, they do offer the hope that, just as society has become unequally stratified, so it is possible to make it less so. However, here the questions are the more immediate ones of why do the unequal suffer so much distress? Why don't the poor do better? Why are their children more likely to enter care? And so on.

Irresponsibility

One favoured and long-standing answer is that poor people do have sufficient resources but they don't use them properly. They are 'irresponsible and ignorant'. If I write a newspaper article about poverty or inequality, I will get letters like one I received recently which stated,

> If you don't know that benefit rates are substantially better than they were in 1979, then you bloody well ought to know .... Perhaps you don't think that an extra £20 a week is of any real value. If children die of poverty as you allege it's because their parents smoke too much or waste their money on gambling, etc. And there is a small matter of poor diets.

This tendency to blame the poor for their misfortunes has a long history in Britain and has been particularly popular with the wealthy. David Vincent, in his fascinating historical study of the relationship between the poor and the state, points out that when, at the beginning of the century, the investigations by Seebohm Rowntree established the extent of poverty and showed that a major cause was low wages, *The Times* still thundered that 'the poor were miserable mainly from their own fault'. Far from it, for Vincent shows from contemporary records that many poor people, particularly mothers, were expert at managing on meagre budgets: their lives were a constant round of skilfully deciding whether to spend their small income on food or clothes, on medicine or soap, on the children or on the husband. Yet all the skills of the most industrious, non-drinking, non-gambling families were not sufficient to remove them from poverty and all its adverse effects if their money just was not sufficient (1991, pp. 6, 10).

It is the same today. Of course, some low-incomed parents do smoke, do bet, do go to bingo. Just as many affluent folk waste their money on drink, too much food, visits to the race course and so on. But the evidence is that people in poverty are not greatly different from the rest of society in their basic values and aspirations. Surveying the research, Anthony Heath concludes that the poorest sections of society are very similar to others in their desire to work, to be honest, to care for their children (D. Smith, ed., 1992, chapter 3). The fact is that they just do not possess enough money to improve their circumstances. Consider this diary kept by a friend of mine, Carol Irvine, and published in a national paper under the title 'The Real Voice of Poverty'.

Thursday. The Giro (£61.19) never came till 11 a.m. Kids never had breakfast. Paid my debts which is £5 to the Provvy for Christmas presents two years ago and £5 to a catalogue for a quilt and duvet. Then I spent £4.24 on food, £1.21 on tobacco and fag papers and 80p on kids' pants. Total today is £16.25 so I have £44.94 left over.

Friday. A letter from school saying they are getting their pictures taken. I just can't afford them. Spent £6.57 on food and left with £38.37.

Saturday. Shopping like this: Loaf 45p, milk 52p, two tins meat 90p, 6 lb potatoes 50p, pudding 40p, six eggs 45p, marg 20p, soap £1.00, tobacco £1.21. Total for day, £5.63, now left with £32.74.

Sunday. My birthday today. Clare wanted to buy me a card so I gave her 30p. But all the cards were more so she could not buy one. We spent the 30p on sweets. Spent £5.54 on food, so left with £27.20.

Monday. Had to go to the chemists, £1.40 on bus fares. Bought plasters, shampoo and toilet rolls at £2.57 and spent £4.47 on food, £1.55 on cleaning materials and £1.21 on tobacco. Total £11.20, left with £16.00.

Tuesday. Jim has not got a job. It's not for the lack of wanting. Today his fare to the Job Centre was 70p just for them to tell him there's nothing. That 70p could have been in my kids' pockets. Clare and Doreen had 50p today for the school panto. Doreen ripped her socks at school so that's another pair – and Gordon's – costing £1.38. Spent £6.66 on food today. Went to meeting at the Salvation Army and put in 50p. Left with £6.26. Not a lot, is it?

Wednesday. Spent £1.00 on light bulbs and £4.44 on food. Now got 82p left so I can get the kids a packet of sweets when the van comes. We just get by.

Following Monday. Drew out my month's Child Benefit, £87. I then do my month's main shop. Spent £38.39 on vests, pants and shoes for the children; £1.03 on face cloth, brush and sponge; £2.97 on three toys; £17.00 on new pans (ours were stolen from the window) and tin opener; £15.00 an month's TV rental.

Then into Glasgow to wash-house. It costs £7.10 to do the washing and £2.80 fares. I was ashamed to bring my laundry out in front of people. The sheets were all torn with them being washed and washed. I haven't got one whole sheet.

Two of the kids wet the bed so if it wasn't for the rubber mats I'd need a new mattress. Now the mats are torn. Can't buy them with the £2.71 left over.

Jim and I have been together for six years and always been on Social Security. The last time we went out for a meal together was five years ago on our wedding anniversary. There are things you have to do without. We've never been to the cinema together. I can't go to a shop for my hair. You can't take the children out.

Most of your money goes on food. But my kids hardly ever have fruit. They have vegetables but it's out of tins. Same with meat, not fresh, always tins. The only shop around here is the van and he's awful expensive. I go up to the market where you get cheap bashed-in tins of stew.

Two of the children get school dinners. There have been times in the holidays when they go without a proper meal but I've always managed to scrape up something even if it's a plate of chips. Sometimes Jim and I go without anything to eat.

The other thing is clothes. When I get the Child Benefit each month I go and buy the clothes for the children but it's all cheap stuff and it never lasts. I bought them shoes, not cheap, £7.99 a pair, but if I could have paid £15 they would have lasted longer. For my clothes I go to the second-hand shop. Even there it's quite expensive. It cost me £7 for two dresses and a cardigan. Otherwise I wait for the jumble sales for my pants, bras, jumpers.

The worst thing about living on Income Support is when you can't get things for the kids. My kids can't get to brush their teeth. I went to buy a tube of toothpaste and they wanted £1.15. Just the other day, my daughter came home from school and said her pal wants her to go to her birthday party. She almost went into a fit when I told her that she could not go because I could not afford a present. It hurt me too.

If I see a bottle in the street, I'll pick it up and the kids can get the 10p on it at the van and they can have crisps or sweets for school because it's horrible if other kids have got it at playtime and mine haven't.

I hate what people say because you're on the Social. Some people think I shouldn't smoke. It's not often that I get a whole packet but it's like Valium, it calms me. You get bother around here, I had to call the police because boys were smashing our windows. If I hadn't had my cigs, I'd have done murder.

It makes me sick that film stars and entertainers get so much money. I had a dream a while back that I was the boss of the world. I made all the film stars get a good wage but hundreds not thousands. And people on income supplement got a good income and those that worked a bit better. (1988)

Carol and Jim were not irresponsible or ignorant. They did want to improve themselves, did want their children to succeed educationally. Sadly, their knowledge and aspirations did not, later, prevent them being homeless, being ill, and for a while, having their children in public care. The irresponsibility of those at the bottom of the pile cannot be taken as the explanation for their sufferings.

Hardship

The straightforward explanation of the disadvantages endured by those at the bottom of the social and economic scale is that they are subjected to hardships so severe that their lives – and those of their children – are adversely affected. In 1993–4, an unemployed couple with two children, aged five and twelve, received £115.85 a week from Income Support and would have had their housing costs met; a lone parent with children of this age would have received £88.65. This was at a time when the Family Budget Unit estimated that such families required over £300 a week for 'a modest but adequate lifestyle', when some MPs were complaining that they could not cope on £650 a week (not counting expenses) and the Duchess of York considered she was impoverished on nearly £10,000 a week!

Whether on state benefits or low wages, there is little doubt that poor families have great difficulties in meeting bills, in feeding and clothing their children. It means that frequently they lack basic equipment such as beds, mattresses, nappies, fires, cookers. Of course, not all poor families are without such basic items but those dependent long-term on welfare benefits frequently are. Their lack of essentials was made clear to me when our local Salvation Army captain in Easterhouse took me to his enormous furniture store – Sally Army Seconds. A flow of visitors was there looking for cheap goods. The captain explained that all the beds had gone and he was now having to provide just mattresses for children to sleep on. He added that he felt ashamed that the only goods he could provide for the people, whom he recognized as God's creatures, were often poor quality, second-hand ones which would not last. But the hardship is not restricted to a lack of new and reliable equipment. It is seen in the following.

- Lack of Children's Participation. A number of surveys reveal that children of poor parents, especially those living on isolated council estates, live restricted lives. They 'find it difficult to participate in the normal activities of their peer groups. They miss out on holidays and outings, on visits to the cinema and leisure centres, on bicycles and fast food – all of them things that the majority of children can realistically have a high expectation of enjoying' (S. Holtermann, p. 47). The government's own Family Expenditure Survey for 1994–5 revealed that the average weekly expenditure of all households on leisure was £31.20. For lone parents in the poorest fifth of the population it was a mere £4.78.

- I occasionally take a book to a seven-year-old child who lives nearby. She eagerly accepts it and starts reading and when I next visit will know parts by heart. She has few other books. It is not that her mother is ignorant about the value of reading. It is that she cannot afford them. Children who are culturally deprived, who are excluded from the wide range of experiences enjoyed by others, are soon at a disadvantage at school. They are the ones whose abilities are not developed, who do not succeed academically and therefore are unlikely to succeed in the job market.

- Diet. A study by Jonathan Bradshaw and Jane Morgan of low-income families found their diet too high on fats, too low in fibre, too deficient in calories (1987). A survey amongst another sample reported that one in five adults and one in ten children had gone hungry in the previous month because of a lack of money, that none were eating a healthy diet and that such a diet would have been beyond their financial means (National Children's Home, 1991).

- These surveys just confirm my own experiences such as when a boy came to my door one Sunday night and requested, 'Mum says could she borrow two slices of bread?'. It is not that low-incomed families are ignorant about what constitutes good diet but rather that they cannot afford it. And it is the unhealthy diets that contribute to unhealthy parents who have underweight babies and to children who are so vulnerable to illness and disease. In 1996, a Sunday newspaper obtained advance copies of two research studies on increasing malnutrition and its effects in Britain. It stated, 'They will add to the mounting evidence that deprivation and poor nutrition in Britain is now on a scale unseen since the Thirties and is threatening the health and well-being of millions of children' (H. Mills and M. Bright, 1996). The studies found that malnutrition and other aspects of poverty are linked, with children at the age of six being 5 to

20 points lower in IQ than their peers and, at the age of eleven, being up to 13 cm shorter in height.

- Inferior Housing. It is poor families who are most prone to damp, overcrowded dwellings often with dangerous balconies and no gardens. It is poor families who cannot afford the heat to warm them. It is poor families who then have their health further undermined by their living conditions. Research has now established that such conditions are linked with many respiratory diseases and infections. Further, the inadequate kitchen facilities, poor lighting, and overcrowding have a high correlation both with accidents and fires (V. Kumar, 1993, chapter 3). Perhaps most seriously affected are those families in temporary accommodation which have high levels of overcrowding and dampness. A report by Shelter and the Scottish Association of Health Visitors revealed nearly 50 per cent of the children experienced deterioration in health after moving into such accommodation.

- Debt. Debt is now widespread amongst families with low incomes. A study of the long-term unemployed by Jonathan Bradshaw and Hilary Holmes found over 90 per cent owing money and paying back an average £10.35 a week (1989, p. 44). They did not owe for houses or cars or luxuries but for clothes, furniture, cookers, even food. It appears that many on low incomes can just about make ends meet but, even if good at budgeting, cannot save. They are therefore unable to cope with the more unexpected demands of the cooker blowing up, the washing machine breaking down, holes in shoes, the children wanting to go on a school trip, the costs of travelling to a relative's wedding or funeral. They therefore look for credit.

- Until 1988, those dependent upon state benefits could claim grants known as Single Payments. The abolition of most grants and their replacement by official Social Fund loans has meant that claimants repay by having their loan taken from their weekly giro. In 1991, some 443,000 people were repaying an average of £5.53 a week. However, Social Fund loans are discretionary and many do not obtain them either because their local office has run out of money or because officials consider they are too poor to pay back. Consequently, poor families have turned even more to other sources of loans. Usually banks do not lend to those at the bottom of the social scale. Indeed, banks and building societies are withdrawing from the inner cities and council estates. Those desperate for cash or goods therefore may turn to legal money lenders and catalogue firms who charge high interest rates which also often ties the recipients to purchasing shoddy goods. Even worse are the illegal loan sharks who may charge 50 per cent or more interest a week with payments enforced by violence.

- A couple living near me took out a loan for Christmas presents for their six children. Unable to keep up the soaring repayments, they found themselves owing £3,000. They have both taken low-paid jobs doing seventy-two hours a week which involves one exhausted parent coming in to look after the children while the other departs for work. They are now just able to maintain payments but the emotional and physical strains on the family are enormous.
- A man came to me to confess that he had stolen my wallet while in our flat. As way of explanation he showed me his knee, smashed in by a loan shark's baseball bat. He had taken out a loan to purchase goods for his children and had been punished when he fell behind on his payments. He stole to avoid another beating. It is not claimed that such beatings occur on a large scale. None the less, there is little doubt that the paying back of loans creates further material distress for families whose weekly incomes are reduced still further and some evidence that they create tensions within families which add to marital and relationship problems.

Material hardships thus contribute directly to poorer health, educational underachievement and emotional tensions. They can also adversely affect parental care of children. In their seminal research, Harriett Wilson and Geoffrey Herbert compared large families in long-term poverty with their more prosperous counterparts. They found that the two groups of parents held similar views about child-rearing methods and similar hopes and aspirations for their children. Yet the former did indeed display child care practices which handicapped their children's social and educational development and which did increase their chances of reception into public care.

What happened? Faced with continuous and almost overwhelming hardships, the parents were pushed into practices which they really wished to avoid. For instance, in flats with paper thin walls, a premium was put on keeping children quiet. Parents, after instructing their children to keep quiet, often avoided noisy conflict by bribing them with sweets or crisps in order to keep the peace – inconsistent discipline. With no gardens, parents in over-crowded rooms often allowed children to play in the streets from an early age so that it became their habit to spend much time out-side of the home. Unable to afford educational toys or leisure trips, the children lacked stimulation and often fell behind at school. Parents after initial enthusiasm for education, gradually withdrew from contact with the educational institutions. The children, street-wise but not school-wise, often met problems with authority figures from the educational, social work and police agencies. Thus, much more than families sheltered from material deprivations, these families became subject to official investigations and interventions (1978).

Inequality Breeds Inequality

Clearly, severe and continuous hardships have a direct connection with the physical, social and educational disadvantages suffered by poor families. Yet, in addition to actual material hardship, there is now evidence that the relative differences, that is, the inequali-ties, between different sections of the population, add to the dis-advantages. Sally Holtermann points to the growing evidence that it is not the richest countries which have the best overall health but the most equal. She cites the 1993 study by Wennemo who, looking at infant mortality in eighteen industrialized countries, found a relationship between low levels of relative deprivation and low levels of infant mortality. Similarly 'a combination of high unemployment and low unemployment benefits was associated with particularly high mortality rates, and a high level of family benefits was associated with low infant mortality rates' (p. 121).

Richard Wilkinson in an article in the *British Medical Journal* (1992) and in an incisive pamphlet published by Barnardos (1994) comes to similar conclusions. He explains that 'the countries with the longest life expectancy are the ones with the smallest spread of incomes and the smallest proportion of the population in relative poverty' (1994, p. 16). Again in regard to infant mor-tality, 'health is affected more by relative than by absolute income levels' (p. 24).

But it is not just health. He concludes about Britain, 'As relative poverty has increased, reading standards have fallen', a decline which is most marked 'in deprived areas during the years when relative deprivation increased most rapidly' (p. 23). Increasing inequality is also associated with the numbers of children placed on child protection registers and removed into public care. Perhaps most striking, he found in Britain that 'the long-term rise in crime ... has accompanied a long-term increase in relative poverty' whereas, for instance, in Japan there has been a long-term decline in income differentials and crime (p. 48).

Wilkinson asks the crucial question, Why do inequalities lead to such physical and social distress? He explains in terms of what he calls psycho-social mechanisms. Take stress. Clearly people in poverty suffer the stress of trying to cope with inadequate incomes. In addition, they suffer the stress of knowing that they are at the bottom of the pile in a society in which so many are affluent. In a society in which many are successful, they see themselves as failures. They feel that they are excluded from the benefits and opportunities which others are grasping. They believe that they count for little at a time when many others are improving their status and importance. Self-esteem is undermined in a nation which exalts money as success. These experiences are internalized and then affect behaviour in adverse ways. Those who see themselves falling further and further behind may conclude 'What's the point?', 'I give up', 'You can't win', and then react with apathy, withdrawal, defeat or anger. The mixture of these feelings and behaviours are manifested in, for instance, parents having less energy to spend time with their children, youngsters losing their educational motivation, adults seeing little point in looking for work, and all having such low opinions of their own worth that even the preservation of their health becomes unimportant. At the extremes, some seek alternative and more achievable satisfactions and status in drugs and crime.

Wilkinson is not saying that all ill-health, poor educational performances, tensions within families, etc. are due to inequality alone. Clearly there are a multiplicity of factors. It must also be added that in the face of adversity, some people fight back individually and collectively. What he is saying is that Britain has created a society in which vast numbers of poor citizens are considered of little worth so that it does not matter if they fall further and further behind the rest of the population. These inequalities then trigger, in some, psycho-social mechanisms which have even more disastrous outcomes for them. He sums up,

> That inequality should have such powerful psycho-social effects shows the crucial importance of the wider social dimension of human life. We are not merely economic beings, with material needs, motivated by material gain . . . . Vitally important is the way in which we fit into a wider structure of meaning, fulfilling roles from which we derive a sense of self-worth and experience ourselves as valued members of society. (1994, p. 68)

Christians who acknowledge the unique value of all God's creatures cannot tolerate a system which, because of inequalities, undermines and dehumanizes some human beings in the way Wilkinson describes. The implication is that it is not enough for Christians to strive for the alleviation of poverty, they must work for a more equal society. Significantly, in late 1996, Wilkinson drew together his and other researchers' studies in his book *Unhealthy Societies*. He concluded that a reduction in income differentials would not only improve national health, not only reduce death rates, but would also improve social cohesion and lessen violent crime. Moreover, far from harming national productivity, smaller differentials actually improve it.

Excuses

The explanation put forward in this chapter is that sections of the population experience grave social disadvantages because unequal conditions push them into adverse circumstances and behaviour not endured by others. It will provoke the criticism that it undermines the notion of self-responsibility, that it is making excuses for the spongers, the work-shy and the criminal. In his book *The Corrosion of Charity*, Robert Whelan takes me to task. Under the heading 'Professor Errant', he writes,

> The exponent *par excellence* of the view that the system is to blame is Bob Holman . . . his unwillingness to confront the moral failings of the poor who surround him is remarkable. He wrote an article for *New Statesman and Society* in which he concentrated on his experiences with one particular family, consisting of a lone mother and seven children, which was so dramatically dysfunctional that it made *Crapston Villas* look like *The Waltons*. He concluded his depressing tale of fecklessness,

selfishness, violence and drug abuse by saying: 'I like them and I believe they should have a fairer deal in an unjust and unequal Britain.'..... There is apparently no need for people to change, all that is necessary is for society to give them 'a fairer deal'. (1996, pp. 79–80)

From the comfort of the offices of the Institute for Economic Affairs in London, Whelan confuses a desire to be alongside those in need with an acceptance of their behaviour. The purpose of befriending such a family was to enable the mother – a widow – to manage on a very low income, to divert a teenager from delinquency, to help a young man come off heroin. In short, the purpose is to support a family in exercising responsibility in circumstances in which people like myself – or even the very capable Mr Whelan – might go under.

Let me give another recent example. The project with which I am associated in Easterhouse is encouraging a young unemployed woman to develop her talents. She is taking on responsibilities within the youth clubs, partly because this is of benefit to the clubs and partly because it may aid her in being accepted on a training course for work with young people. On her own initiative, she took three demanding teenagers on a short holiday with a friend of our project – a retired social worker who makes her cottage available to us. It proved a difficult weekend with the boys stealing money from our friend. On their return, the three boys and their parents had to face the responsibility of paying back the money. The young woman discussed with me how she should have handled the situation. No matter what it looks like from the outside, at the hard end this is hardly making excuses, hardly acting irresponsibly, hardly accepting that change should not occur. None the less, it must still be acknowledged that low-incomes, grinding poverty, damp and overcrowded homes, long-term unemployment, do lead to disadvantages which make it more difficult to maintain family life, to keep children from crime, to achieve at school, to find work. A theme of this book is that the attainment of a more just and equal society will enable more families to act in ways which both they and the rest of society regard as responsible.

The Risk of Riches

The poor are physically, socially and materially endangered by being put at the bottom of the equality–inequality league. What of the rich and powerful? Obviously, the high earners, those who own wealth, those in positions of status and authority, are gaining ever more material benefits in our increasingly unequal society. But inequality can also have its drawbacks for them.

'The Offspring of Fear'

Sometimes the argument is put forward that the affluent, by deliberately tolerating a nation which is socially and geographically fragmented, are stoking the fires of crime and conflict which will eventually endanger themselves. Margaret Drabble, herself a well-to-do resident of Hampstead, in noting government boasts about the prosperity of Britain, wryly comments,

> How odd, then, if this is so, that we should be so nervous of walking in the streets at night or taking public transport of an evening. Should we not feel safer, more protected in the citadel of our own money? We are not, we know, and we know, although we do not admit it, that we live in a society so unjust and unequal that groups within it declare unofficial war on other groups . . . . What are the growth industries now? They are the offspring of fear. Private health insurance, private hospitals, burglar alarms, barbed wire, guard dogs, fortress architecture – these are the fruits of our profit and progress . . . (1988, p. 5)

Drabble is right that the multiplying inequality of Britain has pushed those at the top to spend more on self-protection. They can afford to do so and hence they gain safety in ways not available to those residents on the estates and inner cities where crime is at its highest. As in most matters, it is still poor people who suffer.

Missing Deeper Satisfactions

So increasing fear is a mark of an unequal society but not one felt just by the citizens of the likes of Hampstead. However, there are other dangers which seem to have special application to those who have the financial security of very high incomes and possessions, those who become addicted with getting to the top, of possessing the most income, wealth, status and power.

No doubt, the beneficiaries are laughing all the way to the bank. Yet I reckon that those who have surrendered themselves to the gods of material and social achievement are also losers. They will never be satisfied. A classic example is Peter Robinson, the former chief executive of the Woolwich Building Society. He relentlessly pursued his way to a £300,000 salary, a £450,000 luxury home, a chauffeur driven car, holidays in Barbados. Yet the more he got, the more he wanted. According to an article in *The Guardian*, 'he charged the purchase of a Range Rover to the company' and used company gardeners on his own three-acre grounds (1996). Apparently, he was driven by a desire to be as rich as two brothers who were even more successful. When society revolves around values which glorify inequality, then it sets up a lust which can never be fulfilled.

Moreover, in pursuing the lust for material gains, the pursuers can miss out on deeper sources of satisfaction found within human relationships. In a feature on the trauma of divorce, a forty-five-year-old divorcee wrote,

> We had been married for six years when it all started to go wrong. I think it was the culmination of having spent the best part of the eighties striving for material things. We had built up our businesses and then sold them, had bought a big house in London and then put everything into the children until we had nothing left for ourselves. Having been briefly united by this ghastly rat race – the need to achieve and get on – we found we were totally incompatible. (M. Cantacuzino, 1996)

A top corporate financier earns over £625,000 a year. He is in his office by 7.30 a.m. and may not get home until after midnight. His great delight is in doing a financial deal, 'I feel so good, so fantastic. There's nothing like it.' He is married with four children and his obsession with financial deals meant that he missed spending the summer and Christmas holidays with them. 'But', he says, 'they have a good lifestyle. We can buy everything we want – except time' (N. Gerrard, 1996). This is not to deny that an adequate income does make marriage easier, not to pretend that some high-incomed couples may make good marriages. It is not to deny that an adequate income makes it easier to bring up children, not to claim that affluent parents do not love their children. Yet the theme of these articles reflects the experiences of others, namely that those who get hooked on being at the top financially may well be sacrificing the quality of their relationships with partners and children. In an unequal society, both those with too much and those with too little are put at emotional risk.

From Altruism to Selfishness

The yearning to be at the top, to be superior to and distanced from the masses, can also divert people away from what were noble aims, can entice them from altruism to selfishness. I recall people I knew as a young academic some thirty years ago. They were the radical activists who called for 'power for the people', 'local control', 'participation by the poor'. They were the ones who condemned the welfare fat cats and advocated living in the inner cities next to the socially deprived. But radicalism went out of fashion and was replaced by the ethics of the market place. And some of those radicals proved broken reeds who bent before the winds of inequality and now themselves dwell in affluence and are numbered with the important and wealthy figures of this world. Now they see no wrong in constantly adding to their possessions in a land in which some cannot afford to get their cooker repaired. Now they prefer to travel first class in order to distance themselves from the rabble. Their commitment to others, their readiness to be spent in the pursuit of a fairer society, their willingness to share, have been sacrificed on the altar of inequality.

In like manner, in July 1996, most MPs voted themselves a 26 per cent increase in their salaries to £43,000 plus considerable expenses and perks. Cabinet ministers considered their £69,651 too small and voted a rise to £103,000. The increases were taken from public funds. In the same week, the Department of Social Security announced that, in order to save public expenditure, it would close a free telephone service despite the fact that it was used yearly by 3 million of the poorest people in Britain and despite the fact that an estimated £6 million of benefit is not claimed each year. This change, along with other cuts in welfare benefits, caused hardly a flicker amongst MPs, although, in the past, a number had expressed concern for the poor. In the face of their own greed, they were prepared to increase inequality. Their once noble concern for others was crushed.

On a TV programme in September 1996, the government minister, Ann Widdecombe, stated that, as a Christian, she supported her party because 'the gospel clearly teaches individual responsibility' and that her party's backing of the free market and individual enterprise along with the cutting of taxes allowed individuals to prosper materially and so help others rather than relying on the state. Of course, individuals should help others but the minister overlooked the obvious fact that the same government's policies had promoted so much unemployment and poverty that many citizens were denied the opportunity to be materially generous towards those in need.

Even more pertinent to this discussion, evidence does not suggest that the personal accumulation of riches makes individuals more responsible. They do not become more caring towards, more involved with, the socially deprived. Rather they are more likely to exercise individual selfishness, to want yet more for themselves, to condemn those in need, and to distance themselves from them. Martin Luther King, in a sermon on the rich fool, declared,

> The rich man was a fool because he failed to realize his dependence on others. His soliloquy contains approximately sixty words, yet 'I' and 'my' occur twelve times. He has said 'I' and 'my' so often that he had lost the capacity to say 'we' and 'our'. A victim of the cancerous disease of egotism, he failed to realize that wealth always comes as a result of the common-wealth. He talked as though he could plough the fields and build the barns alone. He failed to realize that he was an heir of a vast treasury of ideas and labour to which both the living and the dead had contributed. When an individual or a nation overlooks this interdependence, we find a tragic foolishness. (1975, p. 69)

Whether drawing huge salaries from politics, industry, financial institutions or welfare agencies, those at the top will regard themselves as smart, as winners, as those who have secured the high incomes and pensions in contrast to the losers who endure poverty. Yet, in God's judgment, they are foolish losers. They have lost ideals which were noble. They have also abandoned the satisfaction of striving with others for a better, more equal society, of co-operating with other human beings in building not a larger barn for themselves but constructing many more smaller barns for the well-being of others. The rich young ruler, who could not obey Jesus' request that he abandon his wealth, give to the poor and follow the master, went away sorrowing. He was to miss a future which could have been spent in fellowship with other followers striving for a noble objective. He was also endangering his relationship with God.

Endangering Our Relationship with God

In the Old Testament, the prophets often urged God's people to care for the poor. Sometimes, when their advice was not heeded, their urgings deepened into warnings. Amos, in particular, detailed their fate. J. A. Motyer, in his commentary on Amos, declared,

> Nothing is left for those who turn their faces away from the needy – or who exploit the needy for their own gain – than that God will turn His face away from them. This is the grim but biblically realistic truth of Amos 8:1–10. The plumb-line hangs vertical in the unmoving hand of God, a mute summons to eternal wrath to flash forth, terrifyingly, disastrously, unendingly against those who are pitiless towards the poor, the central evidence of false religion and dead faith. (1974, pp. 183–4)

In short, making an idol of personal material gain while allowing others to be in poverty can endanger our present and future relationship with God.

The New Testament is not replete with condemnations of the poor. Rather it contains a surprising number of warnings to the wealthy. As the disciple, John, wrote, there is an 'arrogance based on wealth' (1 John 2.16). Those at the top of the affluence and power league can be enticed into the pride of thinking that they are superior to others and, indeed, that they have no need of God. They thus live in opposition to the great commandment to love God and to love our neighbours who, in God's eyes, are all of equal worth. In the parable of the sower, Jesus explained that some receive the seed, that is, hear God's word, but 'the false glamour of wealth and evil desires of all kinds come in and choke the word' (Mark 4.19). Even more strongly, the Son of God warned, 'You cannot serve God and Money' (Matthew 6.24); and 'Truly I tell you: a rich man will find it hard to enter the kingdom of Heaven. I repeat, it is easier for a camel to pass through the eye of a needle than for a rich man to enter the kingdom of God' (Matthew 19.23–4). When the disciples expressed astonishment, Jesus did add that nothing is impossible with God. None the less, his advice is still, 'Do not store up for yourselves treasure on earth .... For where your treasure is, there will your heart be also' (Matthew 6.19–21). There seems little doubt that the desire to possess far more than others – regardless of the adverse effects on our neighbours – is a major force coming between human beings and their creator. Those who are in its grip, those who have made worldly success their god, should listen to Jesus' statement, 'If you are not prepared to leave all your possessions behind, you cannot be my disciples' (Luke 14.33).

People like myself, who are opposed to the inequalities of our society, must beware that we do not enjoy the spiritual plight of the rich. If so we become another version of the Pharisees for we regard ourselves as more socially holy than them. The Gospels tell us that Jesus loved the rich young man. We should long for the destructive and deathly fingers of inequality to be loosened, partly out of a love for those at the bottom of society who suffer its material and physical disadvantages, and partly out of a love for those at the top who suffer its spiritual disadvantages. If we love God then we should want that all his creatures should enter into a knowledge of and a friendship with him.

Nothing in this chapter is meant to imply that human beings should not work, cultivate, produce. God wants his world to be fruitful. But it is fruitful for all. Nobody could accuse John Wesley of not toiling hard yet, at the end of his life, he recorded that he left no money in his will because he had none. Wesley did earn money but he did not accumulate personal wealth. In 1770, he declared, 'The dangers of prosperity are great . . . . If poverty contracts and depresses the mind, riches sap its fortitude, destroy its vigour, and nourish its caprices' (E. Urwin and D. Wollen, eds, 1937). Those who make the personal attainment of money their main goal do great harm to those who are denied a share, to those who are forced into the lower reaches of material inequality. They also do harm to themselves for they are warping their own characters and endangering their own relationship with God.

4

————◁▷————

The Equal Society

So far this book has demonstrated the extent and disadvantages of inequality while arguing that Christians should both practise equality and also put the case for a more equal society. But what is meant by equality and a more equal society?

The Removal of Social Handicaps

As John Rawls pointed out, a strict definition of equality implies an equal distribution of all primary goods (1972). I am not advocating a society in which all people receive exactly the same income, wear uniform clothes and dwell in identical houses. Indeed this would not resemble equality, for people have different needs.

Nor do I regard an equal society as one in which no authority or order prevails or as one in which no differences of function exist. On the contrary, the institutions of industry, education, welfare, law, politics, etc. must have positions within which important decisions are made and implemented. Richard Tawney, in his famous book *Equality*, reasons that equality is not incompatible with certain social differences. He wrote,

> It is possible to conceive a community in which the necessary diversity of economic functions existed side by side with a large measure of economic and social equality. In such a community, while the occupations and incomes of individuals varied, they would live, nevertheless, in much the same environment, would enjoy similar standards of health and education, would find different positions, according to their varying abilities, equally accessible to them, would intermarry freely with each other,

53

would be equally immune from the more degrading forms of poverty, and equally secure against economic oppression. (1938, p. 62)

So differences of position, authority, skill, function are necessary. But in an equal society they should be open to a far wider range of people and should not involve enormous differences of pecuniary reward. Further, the way positions are filled and the kind of decision-making powers allocated to them should be open to challenge and debate. Interestingly, Tawney indicates that access to more powerful and responsible positions can only be widely spread if poverty is eliminated. This difference between equality of opportunity and equality of outcome has recently been revived.

Opportunity and Outcome

Roy Hattersley MP went into print to criticize New Labour for dropping the pursuit of equality (1996). The Shadow Chancellor of the Exchequer, Gordon Brown, responded with an article which claimed that his party wanted a different kind of equality from that of Old Labour. Hattersley had made the case for an 'equality of outcomes', that is for government policies which would drastically reduce differences in incomes, ownership of wealth, housing conditions and so on. Brown complained that such outcomes could only be attained by higher income tax which would be electorally disastrous. He therefore argued for 'equality of opportunity' with improved nursery education, schooling, further education and training which would equip young citizens for better jobs as the gateway to better incomes and conditions. He claimed that this approach addressed 'the root causes of inequality and poverty' (1996).

If Gordon Brown did promote equality of opportunity via large scale improvements in day care, education and training, then these too would probably have to be financed from the public purse. Initially, the advancement of equality – of whatever kind – will require more expenditure. Further, Hattersley does seem to have research findings on his side when he claims that young people are less likely to take advantage of education and training if they have been raised in circumstances of social deprivation. It follows that equality of opportunity partly depends on the precondition of equality of outcomes – the point made by Tawney. At least both MPs are in agreement that a more equal society is one in which social disadvantages are removed so that all citizens can develop their own abilities and also contribute to the well-being of the nation. This brings me to my understanding of equality.

Allowing Human Relationships to Flourish

I regard an equal society – or more accurately a more equal society, for perfect equality cannot be attained – as one in which resources and opportunities are so distributed that some members do not suffer the social handicaps and disadvantages which have been portrayed in previous chapters. This is not to say that no differences would exist between citizens but rather, as Margaret Drabble explains, 'Surviving inequalities will be of such an insignificant and unobtrusive nature that they will not disturb the harmony and cohesion of social bonds' (1988, p. 1). As the Church of Scotland Working Party well concluded,

> God in Christ gave himself for all equally and the heart of Christian ethics is to love God and your neighbour as yourself. The neighbour is to be treated as an equal, with his needs and interests put on a par with one's own. This has clear distributional consequences. Absolute equality of resources is not demanded, but there must be such a redistribution as will allow human relationships to flourish. An insistence upon a more equal sharing of goods within the community is one important way in which we can recognise the status and claim of the other people God has given us to care for and love. (D. Forrester and D. Skene, eds, 1988, p. 68)

The Income Ratio

An equal society, then, is when the distribution of income, wealth, housing, education, training, and so on, do not weigh the odds so heavily against one section of the population that they are channelled into much greater likelihood of ill-health, poor achievement, social distress, unemployment, etc. in contrast to other sections which are placed on the lines leading to financial, emotional, physical and psychological security and success. And it is a society in which wealth, income and power are not so concentrated in a minority that their worldly privileges actually become a danger to them.

But what is an income sufficient to give most individuals the probability of enjoying social advantages and avoiding social disadvantages? It is impossible to be precise. However, Barbara Wootton has grasped the thistle and looked favourably at Sweden in 1976 when post-tax earned incomes of almost all persons fell within a ratio of one to two and a half. She continued that 'a ceiling on personal ownership of capital would also seem logical' (1976, p. 12). Wootton added that 'I should like all differentiation in titles and modes of address to be abolished' (p. 12). This plea now seems to come oddly from one who was a member of the House of Lords. The Lords, however, is just the tip of a social system which bestows privileges upon those born into 'top drawer' families or educated at private schools and Oxbridge. In a more equal society, the privileges associated with these elites would no longer exist.

Mutuality

But redistribution alone is not enough. If by a sudden *fiat*, Barbara Wootton's vision came true with incomes and wealth in a narrow ratio, with decent housing and education for all, with pretentious titles abolished, the result would be a better society but it would still not constitute my understanding of the equal society. For it also depends on a population which wants equality.

I am a football freak. In my boyhood days, I was taken to see West Ham United every Saturday to support the first team and the reserves. Now, in Glasgow, I watch many different teams, whether it be joining the 250 who loyally shout for nearby Albion Rovers or the massive crowd of over 40,000 at Glasgow Rangers. Whatever the game, I know that a good match requires two teams who are well matched in skills and fitness and who know the rules. These are the conditions of an enjoyable game. It also needs players with the right beliefs and attitudes, who want to keep the rules, who believe that it is more important to play fairly than to injure an opponent, who play unselfishly for the team and so draw out the abilities of others, who display sportsmanship. In like manner, the equal society requires not just a fair distribution of goods, the right conditions. Also necessary are participants whose beliefs and attitudes favour such a society.

Fraternity?

How can these beliefs and attitudes, that is those deeply held principles which shape conduct, be described? Richard Tawney was raised in imperial India and then in Edwardian Britain where he enjoyed the privileges of attending Rugby public school and Balliol College, Oxford. From his youth, he mixed with the nation's top politicians, commercial giants and leading academics. Yet he experienced unease about the deep social divisions within Britain and he sought to find and define a bond, a relationship, a spirit, that would heal not hurt, that would unite not fragment. During the First World War, he enlisted as a private and was later promoted to sergeant. His essay 'The Attack' still stands as one of the finest pieces of writing about that war. Seeing men shot to pieces, badly injured himself, Tawney was not one to romanticize about his experiences. None the less, he wrote movingly about the friendships he found amongst his fellow, mainly working class, soldiers. He appreciated their cheerfulness, their willingness to share, their humility, all of which contrasted with the arrogance of the officer class. He saw them displaying something better than the hostility inherent in naked capitalism. He concluded that these ordinary soldiers were driven by something better than patriotism. He wrote,

> . . . they cannot be satisfied with conventional justifications of a sacrifice which seems to the poor weakness of our flesh intolerable. They hunger for an assurance which is absolute, for a revelation of the spirit, poignant and unmistakable as the weariness of their suffering bodies. To some of us that revelation has come from France itself, from women who spoke of mercy in the midst of their desolation, or blessed us as they gave us bread . . . . For an army does not live by munitions alone, but also by fellowship in a moral idea or purpose. (1981, p. 27)

Tawney understood that much of the fellowship of the trenches depended upon the immediate circumstances of the dangers of war. He wanted a fellowship that could be transferred to civilian life, to industry, to the everyday relationships in Britain. Sensing that the soldiers were driven by some moral purpose, he decided that this fellowship for all also had to be derived from some absolute outside of human beings themselves, something that was about love not hatred, about mercy not condemnation, about unity not division. He found it in God.

As his biographer, Ross Terrill, explains, Tawney's principles stemmed from a view of human beings 'neither as gods nor as cogs but as what Christianity knows as creatures' (1974, p. 218). In short, human beings were and are created by a God whose own characteristic is love. Given that God created all people equal and given that God both loved them and wanted them to love each other, Tawney believed that they should be tied together in bonds of what he sometimes called fellowship and then fraternity. 'Fellowship' is a beautiful word closely linked with the way the early followers of Jesus treated and regarded each other. 'Fraternity' had a wider application to include not just the rela-tionships that prevailed amongst that beloved inner circle but also to all of God's creatures. To Tawney, the equality of resources was a step towards fraternity. It did not bring it about but made it possible because it prevented the domination of one part of the population by another and because it brought citizens within reach of each other. As Terrill states, fraternity or fellowship is 'right relationships among free and equal individuals' (p. 217). It implies human beings treating each other correctly, sharing resources, loving each other, because all are brothers, because all have the same Father.

Comradeship

Readers of Tawney cannot help but note that he tends to write about 'men' not 'men and women'. The very term fraternity derives from the word for brother. It follows that fraternity is not a satisfying term for those who want to describe the attitudes and relationships within a society in which women as well as men are equals.

George Lansbury was perhaps an even more remarkable figure than Tawney. Born in 1859 in humble circumstances, he spent most of his life in the East End of London. Converted to Christianity in his teens, he soon decided that socialism was the means most likely to lead to a society akin to God's intentions for life on earth. He became a councillor, MP, cabinet minister and from 1931–5 was the leader of the Labour party. While in the latter position, he wrote that his socialism was 'founded on the solid rock of con-viction that it is the will of God that all his children shall enjoy the fullness of life which this world of abundance can give to all' (1934, p. 38). This equality, Lansbury applied to women as well as men. As early as the 1880s, he campaigned with women for their right to be local authority councillors. Early in the twentieth century, he was involved with a body, Day Nurseries for the Children of Working Mothers, which took the unusual – and much criticized step – of founding nurseries in order to allow working class women to take jobs. In 1906, he wrote, 'To me the most important question for the Christians of England to consider is the condition-of-women question' (cited by B. Holman, 1990, p. 66). He wanted social, economic and political equality for women and in 1912, to the astonishment of other MPs, he resigned his seat in order to fight a by-election on the issue of women's suffrage. He lost and then spent years in the political wilderness. A sacrifice he considered worthwhile.

Lansbury enjoyed and often wrote about the close relationships he experienced in the struggle for greater equality. These included bonds with other MPs, occasionally with affluent supporters of the Labour party, with many Christians of all denominations. Most of all, it was with the ordinary men and women in the East End, particularly in Bow from which he always refused to move. They met on the pavement, in the shops, in the co-op hall, in each other's homes. They worked, agitated, marched, campaigned, suffered unemployment, all together. In his autobiography, Lansbury declared, 'Whatever future there may be for me, my most cherished memories will be of the long, long years of work and pleasure, agitation and propaganda, carried out in company with these countless numbers of people, most of whom possess no money, no property, but who do possess the greatest of God's gifts to man, the spirit of comradeship . . .' (1928, p. 265).

Lansbury, like Tawney, had struggled to find a word to depict the shared values, the sense of oneness, the joint action based on a common purpose. He settled on 'comradeship'. Lansbury was always at pains to give credit to his friends and, in the preface to his autobiography, he names over sixty of them – Mrs Savoy, the brushmaker, Docker Waite who campaigned for the unemployed on an empty stomach, Charlie Sumner, a stoker and hard drinker, and so on. Collectively, he addressed them as 'the comrades'.

Comrades is a lovely word and comradeship a beautiful concept. Yet it still does not quite portray what I am trying to say today. The term comrades is too closely associated with one political party. Further, its use was debased in Soviet Russia where different factions might refer to each other as comrades while plotting murder.

Mutuality

As already explained, and in common with Tawney, my starting point is that all humans are created by God, that we are all of equal value to him, that we are all related to each other, we are kin. Jesus took up the Old Testament teaching that we should love our neighbours and expanded it in two directions. He taught that neighbours were not confined to our immediate blood relatives or race but included even those we meet for the first time. Further, he expounded that it included our enemies, whom we were to love as neighbours. Clearly, the injunction to love our neighbours applies to them as well as to us. In other words, it is mutual for they are expected to love us. This does not mean that all people can give and receive in the same proportion for obviously people have different needs and capacities. It does mean that all people can participate in some measure of giving and accepting.

Placing mutuality in the context of equality and basing it on the acceptance of a common kinship, I regard it as containing the following:

- the recognition that we have obligations towards others and they towards us;
- the expression, as far as possible, of working harmoniously together;
- the movement towards the objective of or maintaining of equitable sharing of resources and responsibilities.

Mutuality is a principle, a practice, an experience and a dynamic. It is a *principle* which can guide our behaviour and attitudes towards others. For instance I would not wish my wife and myself to survive on £9,000 a year with our children being highly vulnerable to bronchitis, accidents, low educational attainments and even early death. According to mutuality, my regard for others, my kin, should be so high that I cannot accept that they should be so exposed and treated. The principle is that I both care for and accept obligations towards them, in short that I should love them as myself. Simultaneously, other people should accept obligations towards me so that I too am not allowed to be severely disadvantaged.

It is a *practice*. Principles should not be mere words. Mutuality has to be shown in our individual and collective relationships with others. Further, it is best done in co-operative and harmonious ways. This is not to imply that all collective action has to occur through public or voluntary bodies to the exclusion of private enterprise. It does mean that activities should be undertaken with respect for others and not in a spirit ruled by self-gratification. Referring again to J. A. Motyer's book on Amos, he points out that the prophet did not condemn people for conducting commerce but for doing so in ways which ground the poor into the ground. God pronounced terrible punishment on these selfish business folk and Motyer imagines them protesting that their market practices 'are not even real sins; they are just the way life is lived and has to be lived in this hard world: where's the sin in being a successful businessman? Surely it's a bit hard if religion is going to insist on one losing money to one's competitor!' (1974, pp. 178–9). But in God's economy, the competitor is also our neighbour. George Lansbury for some years ran a wood yard as well as being a politician and he wrote, 'We cannot show our reverence and love of God through crushing our enemy in the dust and forcing our business competitor into bankruptcy' (1934, p. 32). Whether citizens are unemployed, in self-employment, working for private, statutory or voluntary bodies, the principle of mutuality can still be put into practice.

It is an *experience* which is felt and enjoyed in the company of those of like mind. At times I have known it within Christian churches, within struggling political groups, and, in more recent years, within neighbourhood groups in socially deprived areas. It is an experience in which all members feel accepted, in which all are regarded as valuable participants, in which the well-being of all is promoted. For me, these cherished times have tended to be with small numbers. Others have experienced mutuality in much wider settings such as the Civil Rights Movement in the USA. As Martin Luther King has shown, the sense of being a recognized part of a large movement, set on achieving equality, is more precious and more worthwhile than the attainment of personal riches.

It is a *dynamic*. Individuals who incorporate the principle of mutuality into their own lives will find themselves more at one with others, who also apply the principle, even if initially different from them in upbringing, education, accent and circumstances.

But more, the belief in mutuality can be a dynamic which drives them into building the society in which such barriers no longer exist.

In constructing the principle of mutuality, I am drawing heavily upon Christianity. Some Christians might say too heavily and argue that the biblical words apply only to the way Christians treat Christians. Not so. In the powerful parable in Matthew 25.31–46, Jesus tells of the Son of Man coming in his glory and condemning the apparently religious people who did not succour the outsiders – the hungry, the poorly clothed, the prisoners – and he concluded, 'Truly I tell you: anything you failed to do for one of these, however insignificant, you failed to do for me.' There is a breadth in God's mercy that means that the practice of mutuality should apply to all. Other Christians may protest that I am asking non-Christians to take on ideas deduced from Christianity. Yes. Most Christians would agree that, when God instituted the Ten Commandments, he was laying down basic rules for all. In the same way, I believe that the principle of mutuality, derived from Christian insights, has application to all of God's creation.

What of those – perhaps the majority even in Britain – who do not regard themselves as Christians? I reckon that mutuality can make common ground with people of other faiths and indeed of no religious faith. Other religions also conceive of a God who is creator and who exhorts his creatures to love their neighbours. Outside of religion, there are writers, ranging from T. H. Marshall (1965) to Ruth Lister (1990), who draw upon the fact that we are all citizens as a unifying bond. In pleading for mutuality as a basic principle to guide individual and public behaviour, I hope that it has a wide appeal.

To sum up. I suggest that the equal society is one in which resources, opportunities and responsibilities are so distributed as not to place any individuals or sections of the population at severe social or material disadvantage compared with others, and as one in which the principle of mutuality is both widely held and practised. In short, equality entails the proper allocation of resources which allow the development of the capacities of all people in conjunction with public attitudes which make such distribution widely acceptable.

The Advantages of Equality

A Just Society

If greater equality is achieved, what benefits can be anticipated? One is a more just society. This can be best illustrated by identifying some of today's injustices which would be eliminated or reduced.

In a strict sense, justice means having equal access to and proper treatment by the law. At present, justice often depends upon the possession of status and wealth. In 1994, the son of a government minister – himself a strong advocate of law and order – was expelled from a private boarding school for 'school-disrupting reasons'. The police did not prosecute. Other public schools expelled sixth-formers who took prohibited drugs, again without any hint of legal prosecution. In the area where I live, some teenagers were arrested for being rowdy, others for being in possession of drugs. A well-known TV personality is prosecuted for alleged shop-lifting but, with the defence marshalled by a top lawyer, is found not guilty. A poverty-stricken mother, defended by the duty lawyer, is rapidly found guilty of a similar charge and fined. In a better society, the wider distribution of money and the reduction of privilege would mean that no section of the population would receive such favoured treatment and no section would be legally discriminated against.

But justice is about more than prosecutions and court appearances. If all people are equal before God then all should be treated by social institutions with similar respect and dignity. Clearly, this does not happen in today's unequal society. A well-heeled young man from Knightsbridge will be welcomed and served politely when buying food in Harrods and will leave feeling of some importance. A boy I know went to ask a charity for a food parcel. 'How did you feel?' I asked him. 'Like a beggar', he replied. A wealthy tax payer, having difficulty with his returns, can visit the Inland Revenue office, perhaps accompanied by his accountant, where he will be greeted in a civil manner and listened to with consideration, given a comfortable chair, offered a cup of coffee. Those at the bottom of the financial scale can not be so sure of their reception.

While writing these pages, I was approached by a teenager whose employment had ceased and who had been summoned to the Department of Social Security for 2.30 p.m. As he finds it difficult to understand officialdom, he asked me to accompany him. We arrived at 2.15 p.m. to the large, crowded, waiting room. My friend queued for fifteen minutes just to report his arrival and was told to wait. Some time after 3 p.m. he was called into a small room where the DSS official was behind a counter and grill. She did not say 'hello', did not acknowledge me at all, just looked through her papers. She started to speak when a colleague walked in and they had some disagreement over workloads. As soon as he left, the official – without any word to us – beckoned in another colleague and complained about the attitude of the one who had left. All the time, we sat as though non-existent. Finally, she produced a cheque, pushed it at the youngster and said, 'Sign there, you can cash it at the post office.' No explanation of why he had been summoned. No explanation of why the cheque totalled only £21.66, although I was able to work out that it was for four not seven days. Of course, the official was under pressure. Of course, her attitude is not typical of all DSS staff. None the less, it is an aspect of injustice because it is treating in a degrading manner a human being whom God regards as valuable. Moreover, the treatment occurred because the young man was unemployed and from a deprived area in contrast to his counterpart in Knightsbridge. It was injustice springing from inequality.

In a more equal society, fewer people will have to submit themselves to charity or be means-tested by state officials. Moreover, the predominance of the spirit of mutuality should ensure that all citizens are treated as creatures of value whatever their circumstances. If God respects, even loves, all his creatures then justice demands that they treat each other with courtesy, politeness and concern.

But justice is about more than access to the courts, more than being treated humanely by officials. In the Bible, justice often refers to the right ordering of society, to the proper and fair distribution of goods. It follows, as this book has argued, that inequalities are therefore unjust in that they are not what was intended by God, by the supreme lawgiver. Consider these examples.

- Recently, I lent a widowed mother £10 to buy underclothes for her unemployed son – who had no income at all – who was accompanying our youth club on a holiday. The same day I read that Sir Desmond Pitcher, chairman of United

Biscuits was to receive a 21 per cent pay rise taking him to £346,000 a year.

- A long-term unemployed neighbour appeared in some distress. He had taken the initiative to get on a part-time course with the expectation of becoming a self-employed driving instructor. But social security officials had informed him that his unemployment pay would have to be withdrawn as he was 'not available for work'. His choice was to give up the chance of a job or lose the income with which he fed his children. Yet, at the top end of society, people already in one well-paid job are allowed also to take up further part-time posts in government quangos. The chairman of Yorkshire Water receives £120,000 a year for his part-time attendance.

In short, our society is so arranged that some cannot afford clothes while others could buy a few clothes shops without noticing the difference, where some are overemployed and others unemployed, where the government stipulates that the poor should have obstacles placed in their way while their favoured ones should be awarded privileges. These inequalities are encouraged because of a prevailing economic view – which John Gray explains, has 'strong and articulate support in the cabinet' – that an unregulated free market is necessary for prosperity and that the unavoidable spin-offs of the demand and supply market are unemployment for a substantial minority, low wages for many, and very high rewards for those at the top (1996). This economic viewpoint, as will be shown, is open to challenge. But the starting point for Christians is not human economics but God's justice. The Bible reveals a God who decreed that resources should be regularly rearranged to favour equality, prophets who condemned those who paid low wages, a Son of God who lived modestly and taught the dangers of riches, a Holy Spirit who led the early church to share goods according to need. A society which subverts these intentions is an unjust society. By contrast, a more equal society which ensures that all people benefit fairly from God's abundance, that differences are minimized, that opportunities are maximized, is the just society.

To repeat, I do not mean to imply that a just society can depend solely upon laws and regulations which determine the allocation of goods. The Bible also teaches that the law has to be written in our hearts as well as on tablets of stone. Equality entails a population which practises mutuality and it is from this spirit that justice will flow. Consider the contemporary sterile debate about the meaning of poverty. The then Minister of Social Security, John Moore, questioned the very existence of poverty because today's low-income citizens were better off than the Victorian poor. The Institute of Economic Affairs pours scorn on a poverty line set as high as half of average earnings. The essence of these statements, usually made by those who live in comfortable affluence, is to justify policies which give those at the bottom as little as possible. In an equal society, mutuality should conceive a spirit of generosity and sharing to replace the harshness, meanness and selfishness so characteristic of today. In other words, the question would become not how low can the poverty line be set but how can all be enabled to enjoy the goodness of God's provision. The equal society will have mechanisms to allocate goods fairly but these must reflect the wishes of citizens who long for justice for all. Justice will stem from hearts as well as from laws.

A Free Society

The concept of freedom features prominently in the writings of those who argue against the concept of equality. Peter Bauer, in his essay 'The Grail of Equality', says that efforts to reduce economic differences 'would entail such extensive coercion that the society would cease to be open and free' (M. Desai, ed., 1995, p. 209). Milton Friedman entitled his widely read book *Capitalism and Freedom* and argued that only in the so-called free market economy, untrammelled by government rules, were people free to make goods and money as they liked (1962). His ideology greatly influenced some politicians and their supporters in Britain. The New Right, as they were called, accepted that the driving force of human beings was self-interest with Lord Harris claiming that we must accept that personal 'greed' is the reality of human behaviour (cited by M. Bayley, 1989, p. 45). This greed was regarded as a virtue in that it drove people to work hard within a free market where they could reap high rewards. British governments led by Margaret Thatcher and John Major have succeeded in putting these theories into practice with, for instance, the abolition of laws which protected low-wage earners, the selling of former public utilities to private enterprises, and the reduction of income tax to ensure that high earners retained more money. Some free marketers now make the case for putting the armed forces out to tender and allowing hard drugs to be sold on the open market. The essence of freedom is regarded as allowing market forces to determine almost every activity, such as having private companies in control of nearly all agencies including those for welfare and education, and giving free rein to those companies to pay directors as much as possible. Freedom has thus become defined in terms of the economic freedom of a market economy.

Yet away from the London-based think tanks, away from the stock exchange, away from the offices of the management consultants, and out in the inner cities and the peripheral estates, it becomes clear that, in an unequal society, what is economic freedom for some is social imprisonment for others. A long-term unemployed friend once confronted me as I was about to depart for a conference, 'It's all right for you, you're free to go, I'm a prisoner in Easterhouse.' Some mothers climbed out of our mini-bus as we returned from a day's outing to Largs. Thanking me for driving, one quipped, 'That's it, that's our holiday for the year.' She was not joking. They were at the bottom of the economic pile and thus lacked the freedom to choose a week away in Britain, let alone a month in southern France. Nor had they the freedom to choose private schools for their children, private pensions for their husbands, private medicine for themselves. The Archbishop of Canterbury's Commission on Urban Priority Areas pointed out that thousands of citizens are 'trapped in housing and in environments over which they have little control. They lack the means and opportunity – which so many of us take for granted – of making choices in their lives' (1985, p. xv). Some freedom.

Freedom should not be defined by the kind of economy favoured by one group of politicians and company directors. Years ago, Sydney and Beatrice Webb pointed out that freedom is much more than not being a slave and continued, 'We can, in fact, best define personal freedom as the opportunity to develop our faculties and satisfy our desires' (M. Desai, ed., p. 193). Freedom is when all people can develop their capacities and can contribute to the well-being of others. Richard Tawney put it, 'A society is free [when] institutions and policies are such as to enable all its members to grow to their full stature, to do their duty as they see it' (cited by H. Russell, 1995, p. 54). A more equal sharing of resources and responsibilities will enable more people to enjoy freedom. For instance, if the kind of socially deprived parents studied by Harriett Wilson and Geoffrey Herbert had better houses, environments and incomes then they would have greater freedom to raise their children in accordance with their values, hopes and aspirations – which are in line with those of most parents. If the youngsters I see every day had access to the kind of education, training and careers which are open to the teenagers in nearby affluent suburbs then they would be free to climb out of poverty, to work in satisfying jobs, to own a decent home, to travel, to participate fully in communal life.

The above paragraph describes the free society as an adjunct of equality. Yet the advocates of equality are sometimes depicted as the enemies of freedom, as those who will usher in draconian laws to repress individual initiatives. Certainly, an equal society will curb the excesses of millionaires who own several estates, but it will do so in order to free thousands of others who suffer damp and overcrowded conditions. It may not, for instance, equip the actor Robert Downey, Jr with the kind of income which allows him to spend a reported £14,000 a month on clothes. But it will ensure that others have the freedom to purchase a pair of water-tight shoes. Far from being something which is crushed by equality, freedom is its offspring.

Over twenty years ago, I left a university post to initiate a community project on a council estate. I soon met and became friends with a local young man, brought up in hardship, and by this time, unemployed and on probation. He found an outlet for his abilities in the project, eventually became a staff member, was encouraged to study for 'O' levels, then 'A' levels and then obtained a place at university. Today he holds a senior and fulfill-ing post in a large voluntary agency. His neglected capacities were developed because that project just happened to be located on his estate, close to his home. He was freed. Yet thousands of others are not so fortunate and so never even realize that they have an intelligence and skills which could equip them for careers. An equal society should ensure that they too are freed.

In another sense, that young man was not the only one to experience greater freedom. As a senior university academic, I thought I had freedom and certainly I did according to common standards. I had an academic reputation, high salary, detached house, travelled extensively, could probably choose to move to other jobs. Yet, in a strange way, these freedoms had constrained me so that I was distanced from those in social need and from

God. I think it fair to say that I had become imprisoned by sin. I am not claiming that all professors are bound in the same way but I had to break free. In moving into a different sphere of life, I found a closeness to other humans, the joy of acting with others towards a shared purpose, above all the knowledge of being in obedience to God.

Paradoxically, some need to be freed from deprivation and others from privilege. A more equal society will make this possible for many more. The Revd Tim Scott studied Christian agencies in areas of high urban need and he cited one minister, Trevor Lockwood, as explaining that freedom is 'people being set free to be the kind of people God wants them to be . . . to be free from the enslavement of guilt, sin, poverty, hunger, injustice and oppression, as well as from the corrosive effects of money, possessions and power' (1994, pp. 120–1). Such freedom is not guaranteed but is made more likely in an equal society.

A United Society

Inequality has divided and fragmented Britain. Mention was made in Chapter Two of Will Hutton's analysis that our nation is a 40/30/30 society with the bottom 30 per cent split off from the rest in terms of lifestyle, places of residence, human distress and opportunities. These divisions can be addressed by a more equal distribution of resources which will spread a desirable uniformity in regard to place of residence, health, education and job opportunities. Further, they will help to counter what Wilkinson calls the psycho-social effects of inequalities which can precipitate crime, abuse and apathy. A more equal country will be a more united, more safe one.

But, again, the equal society consists not just in the lessening of great material differences but also in the promotion of mutuality. J. A. Motyer explains that Amos denounced the wealthy not just for promoting material inequality but also for creating social divisions. They treated poor people not as valuable beings who belonged to the human race but as objects, 'a thing to be treated with the utmost scorn' (1974, p. 182) – disunity. History repeats itself today with the powerful sneeringly describing sections of the poor as 'the underclass', pouring scorn on those who live rough, whipping up feeling against single mothers who depend on Income Support. They are regarded as beneath other citizens and to be treated in ways which separate them from the rest of society. By contrast, the spirit of mutuality, because it values all people, will draw them into a more cohesive society. David Donnison writes,

> Egalitarians are often accused of indulging in 'the politics of envy' . . . seeking a more equal world does not feel like envy. It does not even *feel* as if money and material wealth were the central issues. So what *is* it about? It is about creating a world in which people find it easier to see and hear each other, not treating each other as objects; a world in which it is easier to treat other people with respect and kindness, even when we disagree profoundly with them; a world, if you like, in which it is easier to be good and harder to be bad. (D. Forrester and D. Skene, eds, 1988, pp. 3–5).

In such a world, the fair allocation of resources along with the spirit of mutuality will draw people together in common goals and action. The underclass will fail to exist both in terms of a poverty-stricken group and also as that fabricated outgroup which exists as the object for hate. Instead there will be a united society.

A More Christian Society

Not least, I believe that a more equal society will be one more in accordance with the aspirations of Christianity. Richard Tawney concluded that gross inequalities are 'an odious outrage on the image of God' (1981, p. 184). By contrast, one in which God's resources are shared more fully amongst his creatures is less odious, less sinful. I do not believe that the Jesus who valued the poor, who healed the beggars, who drew in the outcasts, wants a society where many suffer needless ill-health, where children are unnecessarily removed from their parents, where many are deprived of good education and employment. Equality will free many from these shackles. Moreover, Jesus warned, 'If a kingdom is divided against itself, that kingdom cannot stand' (Mark 3.25). The unity implied in equality, the fellowship made more likely in bonds of mutuality, are much more in keeping with Christianity than a people divided by selfish greed, obsession with material gain, and attitudes which provoke enmity and conflict. Justice, freedom, unity, all have Christian undertones, all are made more likely within a context of equality. Truly has the writer of Proverbs said, 'there is joy for those who seek the common good' (Proverbs 12.20).

An equal society? Critics will dismiss it as utopian and protest, 'What about sin? That will defeat your ideals. Society is getting more unequal. Mutuality? No chance.' Of course, utopia cannot be obtained in this present age. Sin will endure and so ensure that elements of selfishness, greed, crime and enmity remain. But the case for equality is not based on the expectation that it can eliminate sin. Rather it is based on the expectation that it can further the conditions and attitudes which bring out the best in humankind rather than the worst. Evil thrives in the darkness of inequality. It will have a much harder time in the sunshine of equality. Sharing of goods, allowing all individuals to develop, treating each other in the spirit of mutuality, this is the soil for a better society and a better people.

And the indicators are not all discouraging. A study of 10,000 female respondents, edited by Bernadette Vallely, reveals that a large majority want less hierarchy and competition in the work-place, they desire that employers and employees should be united in a concern for the quality of life rather than in pursuing individual, monetary gain (1996). As women become a larger part of the workforce, their wishes will become more significant. Living in Easterhouse, I regard myself as a realist as well as an idealist. Here, in one of the most unequal parts of Britain, there are people and movements who want a more equal country. Equality can be pursued, as will be shown in the next chapter.

5

Towards Equality

Equality has been difficult to define. I have suggested it involves a distribution of resources so fair that it allows for the development of the capacities of all people, along with the widespread existence of attitudes and relationships which make such distribution acceptable. More straightforwardly, Margaret Drabble writes, 'Only a society which can imagine the plight of its weakest members and legislates for their inclusion into society rather than their virtual expulsion from it, can call itself a just or equal society' (1988, p. 8). Perhaps such an equal society can never be reached, no more than can the ideal family or the perfect marriage. But, at least, the pursuit towards equality can and should be attempted. How can it be undertaken? I do not pretend to have the answers but I can put forward some ideas.

Structural Change

Margaret Drabble stated that society must legislate for change. Clearly the vast inequalities of Britain can only be tackled if democratically elected governments legislate for profound changes in the allocation of income, wealth, opportunities and power. These far-reaching reforms are often called structural reforms in that they would alter the very economic and social foundations of the nation. What reforms are required?

Central Reforms

It is not within the scope of this volume to make detailed proposals. But I have drawn upon two sources. One is from conversations

I have held with poor people themselves in the neighbourhood in which I live. Their views and tone have much in common with an article written by Christine Nolan, an unemployed, disabled woman, married to a man earning £140.80 a week as a hospital ancillary worker. She calls for social justice, 'To start with, a decent living wage; the social contract; access to a new benefit for low-paid workers; highering the thresholds to housing and council tax rebates; ending standing charges on utility bills. To fund these benefits . . . . I suggest a maximum salary for high earners' (1996).

The other source comes from the writings of experts such as David Donnison (D. Forrester and D. Skene, eds, 1988), Tony Walter (1989), Vic George and Irving Howards (1991), Frank Field (1995) and the Social Justice Commission (1994). Their proposals can be grouped in four directions.

First, improvements in opportunities by means of better education and training along with government measures to rapidly increase employment. Second, upgrading living conditions. This would entail a reform of housing finance in order to shift public resources from mortgage relief for the affluent to greater funding for council housing, housing associations and housing co-ops. In addition, legislation to free local authorities to spend receipts from council house sales on building replacement council accommodation. Third, increases in the incomes of those at the bottom of the equality—inequality league by the following:

- a minimum wage;
- a move away from the DSS means-tested benefits such as Income Support to schemes such as tax credits, social dividends or a basic income;
- an increase in levels of Child Benefit which is a popular benefit and which is usually paid direct to mothers.

Fourth, reductions in the incomes and wealth of those at the top by the following means:

- Income tax changes so that it becomes more progressive with high earners paying substantially more than at present. As long ago as the mid-1970s, Barbara Wootton demonstrated how a graduated income gains tax could achieve this end (1974).
- A more efficient wealth tax. Will Hutton shows that inheritance tax, as presently operated, has little effect on the wealthiest families. He argues that the ownership of land,

stocks and shares, family companies, etc. can only be radically redistributed by two steps. One is that the level of that tax is raised. The other is that loopholes be closed: at present such tax can easily be avoided by trusts and tax exile abroad. As one example, he points out that the Duke of Marlborough's Blenheim estates are held in a Lausanne-based trust. He continues that the strict application of a higher tax would fuel a more equal society. A further benefit would be that, as the wealthy had to sell in order to pay tax, so 'it would open up opportunity by allowing young farmers and businessmen to buy farms and businesses . . . so introducing new blood into them and raising levels of productivity . . . . Inheritance tax could be used simultaneously as a means of levelling down and levelling up and making Britain a fairer and just society' (1994).

- A maximum wage, as suggested by Professor Donnison, which could go a long way to achieving the two and a half to one ratio in incomes.

These proposals mainly concern the economic policies of central government. The suggestion for a move away from means-tested benefits would greatly reduce the unpopular visits by poor people to be quizzed, assessed and judged by officials. The improvement of living standards would enable more parents to cope adequately with their children. But the effects of these reforms will take years to achieve and hence it is appropriate to make some brief comments about the personal social services to which many citizens do turn.

The Personal Social Services

In recent years, huge changes have taken place within local authority Social Services Departments (Social Work Departments in Scotland). Legislation has pushed them into placing many of their services for elderly people and those with special needs on to the market. Many social workers have become case managers who assess needs and then negotiate with the independent sector for placements – the contract culture as it is called. Within the realm of families with young children, media publicity about a number of tragic child deaths has led to policies which put resources predominantly into child protection with a consequent decline in the preventative or supportive work which had been a feature of child care social work. One result has been a reluctance by some parents, usually those on low incomes, to approach departments for fear of losing their children. Those who do get into the system sometimes say they receive little practical help but are subjected to checks and observation. As one parent, who asked for help with her children, put it, 'They showed no understanding of the struggle I was having and problems I was experiencing. We were policed instead. They were over-zealous, they undermined, demeaned and devalued the role of us as parents' (cited by A. Weir, 1996).

A lone mother with young children was living in an over-crowded, damp flat. She approached social security for a Social Fund loan for furniture. Her request was refused and she asked me to accompany her when she asked for her application to be reviewed. The polite official was sympathetic but explained that her section simply did not have enough funds to go round. Observing the children, she suggested that the woman approach the Social Work Department for help. The usually passive woman reared up, 'No way, they'll take the weans.' She was frightened of seeking help from social workers. In fact, I know the local social workers were not keen to remove children. Research shows that most social workers regret the decline of prevention just as they are opposed to the system whereby much care is now obtained via contracts with other agencies. They too are victims, they too are being made to behave in ways with which they are not happy.

The personal social services should be run in ways which regard users as of as much value as other members of society. In regard to parents such as the mother I accompanied, their emphasis should be on supporting them to perform adequately the task of looking after and retaining the care of their children. To this end, I propose that the services be characterized by what I call a 'facility approach'. This does not mean that child protection can be dropped, it does mean that the majority of resources – and clearly the departments would have to be properly funded – would be in the form of facilities provided directly by local authorities and voluntary bodies and offered on a neighbourhood basis to families who want to make use of them. As I have enlarged elsewhere, these would include day care provision, family centres, play schemes, domiciliary help and social work counselling (1993, chapter 5). Interestingly, recent cross-cultural research by Matthew Colton and his colleagues reveals that users regard with suspicion those services linked with the removal of children but look positively upon those which provide day care, counselling and information. They write, 'In practice terms, services which are sensitive to local needs and cultures and which are delivered in a spirit of partnership and empowerment have a significantly greater chance of being valued and valuable' (1997). This approach is in line with egalitarian values. The help offered would not impose stigma or fear and would thus avoid the present process by which parents are made to feel inferior to others. Their quality would not depend on the size of the users' wallets. The outcome would be to enable them to raise their children with facilities taken for granted by more affluent families. The gap between them and the privileged would be narrowed.

Change Is Possible

Overall, the proposed reforming strategy is for government investment to improve the life opportunities for those who are now excluded from mainstream society, for economic and fiscal reforms which promote greater equality in incomes, for environmental changes to ensure decent living standards for all, and for the adoption by the personal social services of a facility approach. The objective would be to abolish those destructive inequalities which do so much harm to many citizens. The prospect of achieving profound structural changes is daunting and there is a tendency at present to conclude that only the smallest of improvements can be won.

Yet reflection upon my lifetime shows otherwise. I was born in the 1930s when unemployment was widespread and my own father was periodically out of work. Access to adequate health care was the preserve of those in secure jobs and covered by insurance schemes. The majority of citizens on low incomes resided in privately rented, often poor quality rooms. They were rarely able to afford to allow their children to attend school beyond the age of fourteen. Poor law legislation was still in force with, on any one day, over a million people receiving the grudging help from Public Assistance Departments. I recall the cry of my grandmother, 'Don't let me finish in the Union' – the Union being the workhouse. Then a transformation occurred during the war of 1939–45. Common danger seemed to ignite common concern. The wartime coalition government passed the Education Act

(1944) and the Family Allowances Act (1945). The Labour party achieved power in 1945 and, despite enormous economic difficulties, promoted near full employment, massive house building, and the establishment of the National Health Service. Not least, the National Assistance Act (1948) opened with its memorable words, 'The existing Poor Law shall cease to have effect.' Thus, within a few years, profound legislative reforms did take place.

There is one Act which receives little attention in the social history books but to me is among the most precious of all – the Children Act (1948). It is worth expounding for it demonstrates that values can change and, when they do, they find an outlet in different forms of service. Before the war, the care of deprived children was scattered amongst voluntary societies, various central government ministries and local authority committees. Many of the children were in large and impersonal residential establishments. Public concern seemed to have evaporated with the passing of the great child care pioneers such as Dr Barnardo. Deprived children were not valued. Then came the war and over 6 million children – I was one of them – were evacuated. The arrival of working class children opened the eyes of many in middle England to the poverty of urban children and was one of the factors that led to widespread pressure from all social classes for action against social deprivations. In addition, the evacuation put children on the public agenda. Many were in foster homes and the needs of foster parents as well as those of children separated from their relatives became the subject of study. Local authorities had to open 600 hostels or children's homes for the more demanding evacuees, and experts such as Dr Donald Winnicott made popular broadcasts and wrote articles recommending small units and skilled staff.

The expectation that many evacuees would have no parents to whom to return prompted the government to consider new services for it was recognized that it would not be good enough to put them in the demeaning Public Assistance homes. Wartime campaigners such as Lady Allen pushed the government into agreeing to set up an inquiry into child care. The tragic death of a foster child, Dennis O'Neill, hastened the process and the Curtis and Clyde Reports in 1946 recommended that priority be given to fostering, that children's homes be smaller and more humane, and that a new service should be staffed by workers able to give personal care.

The Children Act (1948) established the local authority Children's Departments with the sole task of caring for deprived children. The Act replaced the Poor Law statute charging authorities 'to set to work or put out as apprentices all children whose parents are not . . . able to keep them' with a clause placing a duty on local authorities 'to exercise their powers with respect to him (the child) so as to further his best interests, and to afford him opportunity for the proper development of his character and abilities'. The child care historian, Jean Heywood, comments that this clause is 'perhaps unmatched for its humanity in our legislation' (1959, p. 158). The 1948 Act represented an enormous shift in the attitude of the public towards children in care and the result, as I have demonstrated in an account of the Manchester Children's Department, was a better service for and happier lives for thousands of children (1996).

The contrast between the 1930s and the post-war period is proof that societal values can alter and can lead to profound reforms. It may be retorted that much of the welfare state of the 1940s has now been destroyed and that its basic principle of service available to all according to need and not capacity to pay has been rubbished and undermined. Similarly, the Children's Departments no longer exist but have been incorporated into Social Services Departments. But all this is further evidence that change is possible. The many proposals to advance equality which are put forward in this section are indeed far-reaching and will come about only if many people change their beliefs, attitudes and practices. But the changes are not impossible.

The Church and Equality

Julian Le Grand stated, 'to change the way they [people] behave, it is crucial to change what they believe. Indeed, ideology can often override self-interest . . . . A change in beliefs can even induce people to reduce their power and privilege' (1982, p. 155). Changing beliefs can have a sinister ring about it if it implies brain-washing and manipulation. But it is quite acceptable if done openly in a climate in which differing opinions can be voiced. Political parties, newspapers, religious groups, trade unions, advertisements and so on are continually trying to mould public thinking.

In regard to equality, changing attitudes and principles is

important for two reasons. One is that the structural reforms necessary to redistribute resources can only occur in a democratic system when sufficient numbers of citizens are prepared to vote for them. The other is that they are necessary in order to weaken the influence of institutions which uphold inequality but which should not be the subject of legislation. For instance, there is little doubt that the public schools are major conveyors of privilege. But I for one would not wish for legislation to suppress them as I believe that parents should be free to choose them. However, if more citizens believed and practised mutuality then more would be unwilling to give their children excessive favours which put their neighbours' children at a distinct disadvantage. Students would be more reluctant to go to Oxbridge knowing that attendance there gave them greater access to certain occupations and positions than people of similar abilities educated elsewhere. The pursuit of equality requires structural reforms carried through by government, institutional reforms shaped by public mutuality, and individual reform which, as will be shown, pertains to people living lives which are consistent with equality.

A Mixed Record

What of the Church in all this? (With the term 'the Church' being a shorthand for the many differing Christian churches.) It is not my intention to claim that the promotion of equality be at the centre of every sermon. The Church has many responsibilities including those of worshipping, praising and glorifying God; building up believers in holiness; being a witness to the God of love, to his Son, Jesus Christ and to the Holy Spirit. Yet there are elements of equality in all of these. God created people equal in his sight and his love for them should be expressed in ensuring that all have access to the abundance of the earth. His Son was at pains to be at one with those in greatest need. The Trinity is a revelation of a community and fellowship which should be reflected amongst human beings. It follows that, as one aspect of its obedience to the Lord, the Church should be prepared to encourage equality. It should do so in regard to the followers of Christ and also in regard to the world at large for Christians believe that God cares about all of his creatures whether they acknowledge him or not.

The Church has a mixed record in the face of inequalities. The

Church of Scotland report *Just Sharing* draws out the egalitarian teaching of some early Church Fathers. Clement of Alexandria (about 150–216) argued that God had made everything for all and continued, 'Therefore everything is common, and the rich should not grasp a greater share.' St Basil the Great (330–79) declared, 'That bread which you keep, belongs to the hungry; that coat which you preserve in your wardrobe, to the naked; those shoes which are rotting in your possession, to the shoeless; that gold which you have hidden in the ground, to the needy.' The theme of these early leaders was that God owned everything and the inhabitants of the earth should ensure that all had a fair share. Thus Ambrose of Milan (about 334–97) regarded charitable acts as restitution, saying, 'The earth belongs to all, not to the rich . . . . Therefore you are paying a debt, you are not bestowing what is not due.'

In succeeding centuries, when much of this teaching was disregarded, there were still examples of Christian movements which bucked the trend by practising greater equality. Peter Aldus of Lyons founded the Waldensians who redistributed wealth within their circle. In England, the priest, John Ball, led a peasants' revolt and was reported to have preached, 'Things cannot go well in England, nor ever will, until all goods are held in common, and until there will be neither serfs nor gentlemen, and we shall all be equal' (D. Forrester and D. Skene, eds, 1988, pp. 91–3). Later, some support for the reformers came from those who looked for a more just society and later still the Levellers were an influential, if short-lived, force.

Yet these movements were frequently opposed by and even crushed by other sections of the Church which increasingly sided with the powerful. Victorian Britain, as Chris Bryant explains, had a number of ministers and churches who sided with the poor and a few who put the case for equality (1996). Generally, however, the churches were not a major force in opposing the gross inequalities arising from the excesses of the free market. George Lansbury was converted both to Christianity and socialism yet for a period he stopped attending church when he became disillusioned with the many clergymen who accepted poverty, opposed state action to relieve unemployment, and condemned low-paid dockers who went on strike.

Whatever the achievements and failures of the Church in the past, our concern is what it does now. How can it make others more sympathetic towards those who suffer the disadvantages of inequality? How can it help to spread the spirit of mutuality so that even the privileged are prepared to back greater equality? How can it stand with those at the bottom as they press for improvements? I believe the Church can do something by changing its own practices and by proclaiming the case for equality.

Practice

If the Church is to promote equality, then it must give some priority to practising equality within its own ranks. At present, in many ways, instead of challenging the inequality of the world it appears to reflect it. It does so in *leadership*. The Church of England, in George Carey, at last has an archbishop who is not a product of the public schools and Oxbridge. Yet its bishops and higher clergy are still disproportionately drawn from such favoured backgrounds. In short, it is similar to the judiciary, the higher civil service, members of the Cabinet. Outside the Anglican Church, Oxbridge is less in evidence but leadership, unlike that of the early Church, is still mainly in the hands of those drawn from comfortable backgrounds.

The inequality is seen in *membership*. Church life should be an expression that all kinds of people are one in the sight of God. As John Stott says, 'God intends his people to be a visual model of the gospel, to demonstrate before people's eyes the good news of reconciliation . . . a single new humanity . . . a model of human community' (1994, p. 111). Sadly, as he continues, the Church has re-erected the barriers of 'caste or class'. Thus many churches are overwhelmingly made up of the well-qualified, the well-heeled, the well-off, those who are in secure posts and affluent homes. Of course, the Church does not want to exclude these members. But the trouble is that having them heavily over-represented has resulted in the Church becoming like a middle-class club in which others feel uncomfortable.

Bob Mayo has written a moving account of how difficult it is for alienated, working class youngsters to settle into existing churches even after they become Christians. Bob and his colleague Eddie Webber were convinced that all are equal before God. Bob wrote,

> There is no middle class and no working class in Christ. Eddie jumped over the fence to avoid taking exams. I took my exams

twice because I wanted to go to university. So what? We were one in Christ. Our two environments could not have been more extreme and different. I grew up in Wimbledon in a lovely big house. Eddie grew up in Bermondsey in a council block. I grew up with six people in a ten-bedroomed house; Eddie grew up with six people in a three-bedroomed flat. When we were actually working together with the young people, class differences were not an issue because we were concentrating on what we had in common in our belief and our commitment to the work. (1996, pp. 64–5)

Bob and Eddie were determined to draw local teenagers into their Bermondsey church. They did so. There were difficulties with existing worshippers and they had to resort to separate services. Yet still the two kinds of Christians clashed and, in the end, the church leaders decided that the new service would have to close. This is not unusual. It is not that church members do not care. It is rather that they have developed a Christianity which is in keeping with the style and language of their homes, education and work. They cannot adapt to different people while the unemployed youngsters could not feel at one with them. The inequalities of our society are so deep, so strong, that sometimes even the Church does not bridge them.

The Church inequality is seen in *location*. The gospel should be for all but its resources, efforts and ministers seem concentrated in the suburbs rather than in the inner cities and are even less noticeable on council estates. Indeed, Britain appears to have its own Bible belt with the prosperous churches in the southern shires and coastline. Sometimes I visit such churches and notice the wood panelling, the thick carpets and the sophisticated electronic equipment. I can't help comparing it with the small church I attend in Easterhouse with its wired-over windows, wheezy organ, tiny office (shared with the credit union) and hall which is full of second-hand furniture.

There are exceptions. Charismatic churches, especially black-led ones, have gained a hold in some deprived areas. In others, older churches hang on thanks to the determination of some dedicated ministers and members. But sometimes even ministers do not want to live in these areas, partly because they do not want their children to attend local schools. Bishop David Sheppard, who spent much of his ministry in tough environments, thinks the Church 'will retreat to where congregations are strongest' (1995).

Not surprisingly, the media presentation of the Church is often that of expensively dressed Christians rejoicing in seaside churches. And at Christmas the perennial image presented by the BBC is of choristers from an elite, fee-paying school singing carols in the luxurious King's College Chapel to a congregation of the privileged and affluent. One can't help wondering if the carpenter from Nazareth would feel at home.

To counter its own inequalities and to promote the equality of the gospel, the Church can and should act in the following ways:

It can open its leadership to a wider range. This will entail removing in-built biases towards those with the 'right' background, connections and accents. It will mean a mind-shift which accepts that the poor and deprived of this world have as much to teach as the powerful and mighty, that the Christianity of the unemployed council house tenant is as worth portraying as that of the famous sportsperson or glamourized entertainer.

I recall visiting a long-term unemployed couple. They had 15p left in the world and refused the pleas of their children to buy sweets at the van. They did so because that night, at the Salvation Army, the woman put it all into the collection. It was the modern widow's mite and I realized that I – who could put in a fiver – had to learn from her. Again, an Easterhouse resident fiddled his electricity meter. He became a Christian and promptly reported himself. The electricity company insisted on a prosecution and he was fined and ordered to repay the arrears. Receiving Income Support for himself, wife and several children, he was in desperate straits when he was offered a job as a butcher's assistant. The low pay combined with the loss of free school meals meant he would have been financially worse off so the butcher persuaded him to work 'on the side'. After two days he gave up as he decided it was inconsistent with Christianity. In this era of parliamentary sleaze, this man's honesty has a message for us all. In future, the Church should seek out and value the message of these kinds of Christians. Noticeably, at Bermondsey it was middle-class Bob not working-class Eddie who was in the ministry. It should have been both.

The Church should concentrate its efforts on those areas where the gospel is least heard. In short, there should be equality of access to the message. The tragic death in 1996 of the Revd Christopher Gray, in an inner city part of St Helens in Merseyside, drew attention to the fact that some clergy are making a

deliberate decision to follow Christ into the areas of greatest
need. The Revd David Kirkwood was a vicar in a prosperous
parish in Leicestershire when he announced he was leaving for
Toxteth in Liverpool. His churchwarden asked him, 'Have you
gone out of your mind?' He moved in with a team and describes
his task as that of 'preaching a forthright, evangelical gospel and
sharing realistic concern through appropriate social care' (1995).
It is not just clergy. Some lay Christians have made the same
move. An example of deliberate relocation by a number of
Christians (in the USA) is found in Robert Lupton's book *Return
Flight* (1993). It is worth adding that such Christians are advised
to present themselves less as missionaries who introduce God to
the new locations and more as servants who go to work alongside
resident Christians who already know God.

The Church can also contribute to greater equality by shifting
its main resources. There is a danger that the Church has its conscience satisfied if a few Christians make forays into neglected
areas or if it establishes some outposts or missions. If it is serious,
the Church will move much of its personnel and wealth there. All
London-based denominations could sell their headquarters and
training colleges and shift them to places where the Church is
numerically weakest. A threefold effect can be anticipated. Local
churches will grow stronger as incomers join. The churches' witness and impact will be more effective. The local economy will be
boosted as clerical and support staff take residence. Overall, the
Church will be seen as being serious about spiritual, social and
material equality.

Proclamation

Following the publication of the Rowntree *Inquiry Into Income and
Wealth* in 1995, Will Hutton was moved to write, 'How unequal
must society become before it touches raw nerves and compels
some response ... the facts about the scale of inequality in
Britain still fail to ignite a popular outcry' (1995). It must be asked
whether the Church is prepared to lead this outcry. In the Bible,
the prophets were prepared to put their lives at risk in their public
condemnations. Amos was courting danger when he condemned
those 'with houses and summer residences, their houses adorned
with ivory' (Amos 3.18) in a land where the poor were barely
surviving. Throughout the ages, some church leaders have been

prepared to condemn the rich and to side with the poor. In modern times, some churches in South Africa, Central and South America have thought it more important to oppose social injustice than to look after their own safety.

In Britain, the voice of the Church has been more muted. It is true there are exceptions. Bishops such as David Sheppard and Roger Sainsbury in the Church of England and non-conformist figures such as John Vincent have consistently shown that biblical Christianity is opposed to the vast inequalities now characteristic of Britain. To their credit, the Archbishop of Canterbury and Catholic leaders have condemned homelessness and, with other denominations, have spoken out against the government's determination to deny welfare benefits to refugees seeking asylum in this country. On 5 July 1996 in the House of Lords, Archbishop George Carey attacked the decline of moral standards in Britain. But, generally, although the churches will sometimes express regret about poverty, they rarely make the case for equality. Perhaps, in the case of the larger denominations, they are reluctant to offend affluent members who support them financially. In the case of the Church of England, calls for equality would conflict with its official links with the monarchy which represents the very apex of material and social inequality in Britain.

None the less, despite the offence it would cause, despite the caustic criticism it would receive from the media, despite the angry protests of some politicians that 'the Church should keep out of politics', I urge the Church to make the proclamation of equality a significant part of its public ministry for these reasons. First, because as indicated throughout this book, this is God's world and the Bible constantly reveals his intentions that its benefits are for all. Second, because rampant inequalities represent the triumph of the enemy of God. John Stott is not afraid to argue that the forces of evil have taken over many of the values of the world. He writes,

> Wherever human beings are being dehumanized – by political oppression or bureaucratic tyranny, by an outlook which is secular (repudiating God), amoral (repudiating absolutes) or materialistic (glorifying the consumer market), by poverty, hunger or unemployment, by racial discrimination, or by any form of injustice – there we can detect the sub-human values of 'this age' and 'this world'. (1994, p. 73)

It is evil when a 'fat cat' takes an extra £250,000 a year on top of his already high income at a time when rickets and TB are reappearing amongst low-income families. This is defying what God intended and hence is a success for the forces of darkness. As the Church of Scotland report put it, the Church must be the prophet which denounces evil. It states,

> It is not a prophet's virtue to tip toe around contentious issues when things need to be called by their true name. The causes and agents of maldistribution must be identified. There must be protest when the ideologists of the day claim 'Peace, peace' when there is no peace, and when economic prosperity is reached at an unacceptably high social cost. Prophets must speak out when freedom for some means deprivation and suffering for others. (D. Forrester and D. Skene, eds, pp. 113–14).

Third, because few if any other voices now make the case for equality. The Labour party, traditionally the home of some egalitarians, is now led by Tony Blair who says he wants a society with even more millionaires. If other movements are silent about an injustice to be exposed and a truth to be presented, then the Church should have the courage to speak.

In proclaiming the Christian case for equality, the Church should be general, specific and positive. *General* in that it should show the overall disadvantages which inequality places on so many people in Britain. *Specific* in that it should name those who are prepared to wallow in wealth while others perish in poverty. It should contrast Michael Heseltine's vast estate, replete with lakes, with the overcrowded, damp tenements which spell unnecessary ill-health for their tenants. It should condemn John Birt, the director-general of the BBC for accepting a £35,000 pay rise to add to his overall £299,000 in 1995–6, at a time when other BBC employees were facing the loss of their jobs. *Positive* in pointing to those who apply equality. For instance, PECAN is a Christian training project in Peckham, London. It has a high success rate with 70 per cent of trainees going on to jobs or further training. The workers, from the managing director to the créche worker, all take the same salary of £13,400. This means that more staff can be employed so that it now employs thirty-three full-timers. The sense of equality and unity is regarded as one factor why the project is so successful. A project for which I worked fixed salaries at that of the average, full-time worker. This meant that users saw the staff as mainly interested in them rather than using their posts just as a means of filling their pockets.

All this is not to say that the Church should identify itself with one political party. Individual Christians may well be members of a political party because they deem that its policies are the most akin to promoting Christian ideals. But the Church cannot do so for these reasons. Its primary loyalty is to God not a political organization. The Church should be open to all and will contain members of a range of political parties – and none. The Church's proclamations will never fit into one political creed. For instance, its views on alleviating poverty may be more in keeping with one party while its teaching about abortion more in line with another. However, the Church should try to influence political thinking and action in ways which are in accordance with God's intentions for the world. As so often, Martin Luther King put it well,

> The church must be reminded that it is not the master or the servant of the state, but rather the conscience of the state. It must be the guide and critic of the state, and never its tool. If the church does not recapture its prophetic zeal, it will become an irrelevant social club without moral or spiritual authority. If the church does not participate actively in the struggle for peace and for economic and racial justice, it will forfeit the loyalty of millions . . . (1972, p. 62)

It may be countered that the Church contains differing views on the desirability of equality. A purpose of this book is to be a small contribution to the argument that the promotion of equality is Christian and should be one of the causes which the Church should proclaim.

Neighbourhood Groups

In his book, *LSE on Equality*, Meghnad Desai brings together a number of famous names who have written about equality – Hugh Dalton, Richard Tawney, Sydney and Beatrice Webb, Lionel Robbins, Peter Bauer and others (1995). Yet, with the partial exception of Tawney, they seemed oblivious to the fact that those at the hard end of inequality are capable of taking action themselves. In Easterhouse, there are over 200 local voluntary groups. The Community Development Foundation estimates that over 2.5 million people participate in community projects. As the term 'community' is now closely associated with the huge organization of the EEC, I prefer to say neighbourhood groups. They are voluntary but are not to be confused with the national voluntary societies, some of which have initiated valuable services in deprived areas. The national societies are usually large in size and staffing, often with highly paid chief executives and professional fund-raisers; neighbourhood groups are small, serving local districts. The national societies tend to have unelected managing committees at their central headquarters, often in London, from which stem long hierarchical layers of control; neighbourhood groups tend to be accountable to local people directly elected by residents.

Following their description and analysis of the activities of the Windhill Community Association in Shipley, Neil McLellan and Christine Flecknoe conclude that neighbourhood work draws its agenda from local people, mobilizes their worth and capacities, emphasizes collective activity, and seeks to assist people to take increased control over their lives (1992, pp. 6–7). Similarly, I define neighbourhood groups as 'the residents of a small locality acting together in projects for the collective well-being of members and their neighbourhood'. Typically, they run tenants' associations, furniture stores, youth activities, credit unions, food co-ops, play schemes, welfare rights shops, community transport schemes, day care centres, and so on. Some involve just a handful of people. The North Easterhouse Credit Union has over 600 members. Dick Atkinson estimates that the many projects in Balsall Heath in Birmingham are supported by over a thousand residents (1994).

What has this to do with equality? Obviously, neighbourhood groups tend to be in inner city areas and council estates where the disadvantages of inequality are most in evidence. The location of the projects and the participation of those at the hard end means that they can play some part in the battle for greater equality.

Practical Outlook

First, neighbourhood groups tend to be practical. As explained previously, those at the bottom of society, the poor, have far greater chances of falling into debt with high interest repayments, of suffering hardship, of their children going into care. Credit unions involve local residents combining in order to save together and then to make loans with repayments at no more than 1 per cent interest per month. The loans are not sufficient for mortgages or cars but they can provide access to a new cooker, a fridge, a holiday. They mean that members are not drawn into the clutches of loan sharks. They give them the dignity of negotiating their own loans as equal members and not as supplicants asking for a Social Fund loan. Food co-ops entail low-incomed people co-operating in order to buy food from cash-and-carrys and markets and then selling to members at prices which are much cheaper than local shops. The small co-op in our district sold bread at 27p a loaf as compared with 50p on the vans.

Day care provision, play schemes, holidays, individual support, can be vital to parents going through hard times with their families. Research into the preventative work of both statutory agencies and neighbourhood projects by Jane Gibbons and her colleagues concluded that 'parents under stress more easily overcome family problems . . . when there are many sources of help available in the community' (1990, p. 162). Neighbourhood groups do not remove the disadvantages stemming from social inequalities but they can offer practical help which enables some families to survive.

Challenge

Second, neighbourhood groups challenge the notion that inequality is deserved. In 1982, Peter Golding and Sue Middleton, in their study, *Images of Welfare*, showed how widespread is the impression that the unemployed are workshy and that people pre-ferred to live on Social Security. This condemnatory view has been boosted by Charles Murray with his popularization of the ugly term 'the underclass'. Murray cites Easterhouse as an example of an estate characterized by an underclass of young men who choose drugs and crime rather than work and young women who choose to be lone mothers (1990, p. 12). The implication is that the affluent have virtues which lead to their privileges while the poor have vices and so deserve their deprivations.

In my book, *A New Deal for Social Welfare*, I pointed out that over 70 per cent of Easterhouse children live with two-parent families, that the unemployed tend to be desperate for work, and the employed are frequently on very low wages. In short, most poor people are not an underclass – but they are still poor. The argument is strengthened by the nature of neighbourhood groups which are in the very areas which the pundits identify with the underclass. They are run by committees and volunteers, many of whom are unemployed, some of whom are lone parents, and nearly all of whom are on low incomes. These reliable activists want the best for their families and communities. Often they regard neighbourhood groups as a means of taking action against poverty, crime and drug abuse. They are not an underclass. However, their reliability, their belief in family life, does not take them out of unemployment and social deprivations. The fact is that inequality stems from economic and social forces beyond the control of the residents at the hard end. The activities and composition of neighbourhood groups thus serve to refute the argument that inequalities are deserved.

In Line with Equality

Third, neighbourhood groups often convey principles and practices which are in sympathy with equality. They show, although in a small way, that personal greed and self-interest do not have to be the motivation for the supply of goods and services. Full-time staff receive modest salaries, volunteers and committee members take no payments. They reveal that participants are prepared to work hard for the benefit of others, that the bond between supplier and users can be one of co-operation. This does not mean that the agencies can neglect efficiency and profit. If, for instance, a food co-op fails to have an income which exceeds expenditure then it goes out of business. But profits are not channelled into higher salaries for directors and managers, are not drained off as returns for shareholders. Instead, they are ploughed back into the group and hence into the neighbourhood.

Further, neighbourhood groups are essentially mutual. Members accept obligations towards others not from a desire to inflate their own wallets but from a recognition that their neighbours are of value. Simultaneously, they expect those neighbours to accept obligations towards them. This mutuality is well seen in credit unions where the very availability of credit depends upon all members paying back their loans.

The spirit of mutuality must not be exaggerated. In my twenty years in neighbourhood groups, I know full well that cliques can form, jealousies arise, blow-ups occur followed by resignations.

Yet I also know that more generally the participants display endurance, a readiness to give of themselves, and an enjoyment in serving others. They demonstrate that mutuality is not just 'pie in the sky' but does happen in practice.

Self-Expression

Fourth, neighbourhood groups are an indication that people at the lower end of the equality–inequality continuum do have abilities and can express themselves. Will Hutton was quoted as being amazed that Britain's vast inequalities evoked so little public response. He continued, 'Part of the explanation is the reticence of rich and poor alike. The rich . . . have learnt discretion about the scale of their income and wealth . . . . But there is an equal and telling silence at the bottom' (1995). This apparent silence is taken as another indicator that those at the bottom end are inadequate and inarticulate and that therefore middle-class radicals must speak on their behalf. Unfortunately, this assumption just becomes a part of the process whereby the former are kept in their inferior, unequal position. *The Observer*, of which Will Hutton is the editor, gives expression to middle-class, often Oxbridge, journalists and academics, not to that 30 per cent which Hutton shows is excluded from mainstream life. Most news bulletins on TV feed the interests of the owners of wealth by giving the latest stock exchange figures and the state of the markets but they rarely mention what is happening day in and day out in local neighbourhoods. Neighbourhood groups challenge this excluded position into which the media establishment casts them. Their members prove that they can run agencies. In their community papers, in their committee meetings, in their negotiations with statutory bodies, they show that they can write, can be articulate. If they could find a national expression for their voice, then it could become a powerful means of persuading the public that they should be regarded and treated as the equals of other citizens.

Moderating Inequality

Fifth, neighbourhood groups can moderate the psycho-social effects of inequality. In Chapter Three, attention was drawn to Richard Wilkinson's analysis of how the experience of inequality can induce feelings of powerlessness, stress and failure which produce reactions of apathy, withdrawal and aggression. Within neighbourhood groups, residents of deprived areas do exert some control over local activities, do contribute to services which relieve stress, do find outlets for their abilities. Of course, this involvement does not alter the power structure within Britain but it can enable some individuals to counter the grinding and dehumanizing effects of inequality.

I recall a dispirited woman whose child had been taken into public care. She turned to our local project and together we were able to get the child home again. The woman then joined the food co-op as a volunteer and eventually became its chairperson. The approval she received from other residents and her success at organizing the group greatly boosted the woman's self-image and confidence: interestingly, these new perceptions of herself were then also translated into her functioning at home with her parental capacities showing a marked improvement.

It is not my wish to glamourize low-income people, to represent them as all good types ranged against the wicked capitalists. Crime, drug abuse, heavy drinking, sexual immorality, neglect of children do occur amongst the bottom 30 per cent of society. But so they do also amongst the other 70 per cent, including members of that illustrious club, the House of Commons. Neighbourhood groups are not all successes and I have seen those which have closed for lack of enthusiasm and competence. But then failures are not exactly unknown in the City of London. The overall message emerging from the contribution of thousands of neighbourhood groups is that many local residents are willing and able to tackle problems, to provide services, to contribute to their communities. In so doing, they refute some of the prevailing views which are used to justify inequalities. Moreover, they run their agencies in ways which are often in accord with the promotion of equality.

The Church in general and Christians as individuals can back neighbourhood projects. Some already do so. The Revd Russell Barr tells of how, when he was a minister in the Garthamlock district of Easterhouse, his church participated in the formation of an unemployed workers centre and an elderly care project (D. Forrester and D. Skene, eds, pp. 10–16). Nearby, another church initiated the formation of a community association. Today the St George's and St Peter's Community Association runs a high quality pre-school day care centre, schemes for elderly people, numerous youth activities, and owns a holiday centre much used by local groups. The Church Urban Fund has directed some cash into local projects. Credit should also be given to Church Action on Poverty which, in recognition that the views of low-incomed citizens tend to be disregarded, brought a number together so that they could discuss their difficulties and make policy proposals. These were then expressed through articles and through a number of meetings to a national audience.

Despite these efforts, neighbourhood groups tend to be chronically under-financed. Ninety-two per cent of grants to voluntary bodies go to the large agencies. Further, as central government has placed restrictions on local government finances so the latter have cut their grants to voluntary bodies. The National Council for Voluntary Organisations reported that local authority grant giving to voluntary bodies declined by £28.9 million in 1993–4. Two colleagues and I worked in Easterhouse for a project which was run efficiently, with under 3 per cent of its expenditure going on administration, and which catered for many children and families. When funds ran low, the local authority indicated it would make a grant but, at the last moment, dropped out as it was facing its own financial crisis. Fortunately, a charitable trust came up with one salary, but one worker had to leave and I had to cease paid employment and continued as a volunteer. Overall, the result is that neighbourhood groups, the ones closest to and made up of those at the hard end, are the agencies most starved of funds.

In 1994, the Social Justice Commission put the case for a National Regeneration Agency to oversee 250 Community Development Trusts in 250 socially disadvantaged areas (1994, pp. 328–32). The proposal was vague and, subsequently, no political parties endorsed it. I feel the Commission had the kernel of a sound idea. My suggestion would be for a centrally financed National Neighbourhood Fund which would allocate money to 250 or so Neighbourhood Trusts which, in turn, would distribute grants to groups in their areas. If each trust received annually around £3 million, this would total £750 million: small beer these days when government departments lavish some £865 million a year on outside management consultants; even smaller beer when the government poured £2.5 billion into the London Docklands Development Corporation of which one result was to worsen 'the plight of the indigenous poor by displacing their homes and awarding them to outsiders' (Knight, 1993, p. 36). The essence of the system should be democratic and local. Members of the National Neighbourhood Fund should be elected by the 250 Neighbourhood Trusts whose own members should be elected from the 250 disadvantaged areas. The anticipated outcomes would be to strengthen and expand neighbourhood groups, to improve the quality of services in their locations, to increase residents' control over their own circumstances, and to give a boost to the values of democracy and mutuality. The Church could do neighbourhood groups a great service if it campaigned for this proposal and so put it on the national agenda.

The Life We Live

The impact of Jesus Christ stemmed not just from his teachings and his miracles. It also came from the kind of life he lived. His attitudes, his practices, his behaviour, were entirely in accord with the values he proclaimed. He told his disciples to be like servants – and he washed their feet. He gave the commandment to love – and he embraced the leper, the prostitute, the outcast. He told the wealthy not to put their trust in money – and he lived modestly and refused to accumulate possessions. In the last, terrible days, he instructed his followers not to use violence – and he submitted to the cross although he could have summoned angels to his aid. His disciples, who were close to him for years, had to admit that he never sinned. There was a loving consistency about Jesus. Even today, I cannot read the Gospels without being attracted to him.

The New Testament likewise expects his followers to show behaviour which is in line with Christian codes of conduct. John, who was as near to Jesus as any person, wrote, 'But if someone who possesses the good things of this world sees a fellow-Christian in need and withholds compassion from him, how can it be said that the love of God dwells in him? Children, love must not be a matter of theory or talk; it must be true love which shows itself in action' (1 John 3.17–18). The implication is that Christians must live lives that reflect their beliefs, partly because this is an aspect of obedience to what the Lord wants of them, partly because their consistent behaviour is a witness that will attract other people to the truth.

History has many examples of men and women who exercised

a powerful influence because they upheld their own principles. Eric Liddell, Mahatma Gandhi, Martin Luther King, are names which spring to mind. But it is not just the example of famous people. As a teenager, I recall being immensely impressed by the modesty, honesty and kindness of a young man who stuck to his Christian beliefs. The effect of good lives on changing others should not be underestimated.

Today the subject of individuals living according to principle is out of fashion. Having occasionally written about it, I know that it evokes sneers about being sentimental, romantic, naive, unrealistic. Back in 1958, Peter Townsend wrote, 'Equality of sacrifice is not an ideal which applies to others but not to yourself. It is essentially personal.' He continued that such application 'frightens and embarrasses the intellectual. He does not want to be taken for a sucker in public' (1973, pp. 21–2). Even more so in the 1990s when praise tends to go to those who can obtain the highest salary, negotiate excessive mileage rates for their cars, go to conferences abroad at others' expense, get a golden handshake.

Yet if little admiration goes to those who live by principle, the newspapers are quick to identify those whose lifestyles are inconsistent with the standards they hold or once held. Three instances must suffice to illustrate the point. *Scotland on Sunday* ran a feature on Sir Gavin Laird, the former trade unionist and general secretary of the Engineering Union. Mrs Thatcher, although a strong opponent of trade unions, made him a director of the Bank of England; John Major gave him a knighthood. He left his trade union post early with a cheque for £40,000, his new BMW car, and his full salary until he reached retirement age. Since then he has taken on a string of directorships and posts in quangos. The article concluded, 'he will not have anything like the financial worries of those still living in Clydebank, the heirs to a way of life that made Sir Gavin a Communist all those years ago' (T. Condon, 1996).

The Guardian did a profile of Lord St John, a former minister in and prominent supporter of the Thatcher government with its strong criticisms of public expenditure and of those people deriving benefit from the state. The article revealed that he was about to start a third five-year term as chairman of the Royal Fine Art Commission despite the criticisms of a recent official report about the lavish style of the chairman who spent £29,000 on car hire and of the Commission which spent £280,000 renting its London premises. In all, the Commission was costing £800,000 a year. Who pays? The taxpayer, for the money came out of public expenditure.

But perhaps *The Guardian* should run a feature on its own regular columnist, Roy Hattersley MP, the former deputy leader of the Labour party. Hattersley, who frequently complains that the Labour party no longer wants equality, wrote in his column in 1996 about the injustices of low incomes and highlighted the plight of one of his unemployed constituents who had a wife and two children and existed on £525 a month. Hattersley was enraged that such poverty could occur in our affluent society and stated that Labour should judge every policy proposal against the simple criterion, 'Would the outcome increase or reduce equality?' He ended by declaring, 'If New Labour does not believe in real equality, what does it believe in?' (1996). Yet when MPs' outside earnings were published, it emerged that Hattersley was at the top of the pile, receiving £104,300 in addition to his MP's pay and expenses. So much for equality.

Probably everyone is a hypocrite to some degree. I certainly am. We should be careful, for the Bible has strong words for believers who are not consistent. In Amos again, the Revd J. A. Motyer draws attention to the fact that God's condemnation was upon people not just because they refused justice to the poor but also because simultaneously they attended services and gave apparent support to a religion which demanded that they love their neighbours (1974, pp. 115–16). But if, as above, individuals live lives which do damage to principles and values then surely the reverse is true. Individuals can live in ways which uphold the principle of equality and, in so doing, persuade others to do the same. I will illustrate with three more examples.

Alfred and Ada Salter

Alfred Salter was a brilliant medical student who won a string of prizes at Guy's Hospital at the end of the last century. After qualifying, the renowned Joseph Lister appointed him to his institute where Salter's research and publications paved the way for fame in academic medicine or a lucrative practice in Harley Street. Instead, he was to choose to become a 'Poor Man's doctor' in the London district of Bermondsey. What prompted his decision?

Decisions

As a medical student, Salter had visited Bermondsey and been appalled at its slum conditions. While at the Lister Institute, he took up residence at the Bermondsey Settlement in 1898 and became ever more attached to its people. Although brought up in a Christian home, Salter was, by this time, a militant agnostic. His religious change owed much to Ada Brown.

Ada Brown felt called by God to Bermondsey where she lived in a working-class tenement. She led the Girls' Club at the Settlement where her gracious personality had a profound effect. Alfred and Ada fell in love and became engaged and, before long, Ada's quiet influence along with the reasoning and argument of the Settlement's leader, Dr Lidgett, led to Alfred's conversion to Christianity. Never one to do things by halves, Alfred applied Christ's teachings to his own life. It was at this juncture, after conversations with Ada, that he left the Lister Institute and rented a shop as a surgery. Soon after, in 1900, the couple married and lived over the shop. Alfred worked prodigious hours but he and Ada always kept 11 p.m. to 1 a.m. as their time together in which they discussed the day's events. Often Alfred would reveal names which needed more than medical help and Ada would visit. In 1902, their happiness seemed complete when they had a daughter, Joyce, and four years later moved into 5, Storks Road, a grimy three-storied building overlooked by a factory. They stayed there for the rest of their lives.

The Doctor

Alfred's first week's takings, at 6d a visit, amounted to 12/6d. But before long his surgery was so full that he took on a partner, Dr Benjamin Richmond. Alfred's biographer, Fenner Brockway, observing Richmond's prize-winning career, stated, 'never before had two gold medalists become partners in general practice – that they should do so in Bermondsey rather than in Belgravia added to the noteworthiness of the event' (1951, p. 25). Still the numbers of patients grew with Drs Stratton, Goldie and Lowe then joining a practice which was run on co-operative lines with the takings shared equally amongst the doctors.

Salter was undoubtedly a doctor proficient in diagnosis and treatment. To this was added genuine concern. He refused to hurry patients and treated all with courtesy. Brockway recorded,

Stories spread of his devotion to his cases and of his kindness: of the stable-boy too ill with pneumonia to be removed, with him he stayed up two nights until the danger had passed; of a girl in the last stages of consumption whom he visited every day however busy he was, although she was beyond medical aid; of innumerable cases which he treated without charge, of many cases which he sent away to the country or the seaside at his own charge. (p. 24)

Dr Salter soon perceived that many of his patients required rest, quiet, country air, the kind of healing easily obtained by the well-to-do but not by the poor. In 1917, he purchased Fairby Grange, a country house in Kent and used it as a convalescence home for the practice and, in the summer, for holidays for Bermondsey children. After proving its value, the Salters presented it to the borough council.

Locality and Sacrifice

The Salters believed in living where they worked. Their commitment to Bermondsey was seen in regard to their beloved Joyce. Alfred and Ada were Quakers and most of their professional friends assumed that Joyce would be sent to a Quaker boarding school away from the threat of disease and the influence of local children. Brockway comments,

But Ada and Alfred, with all their tender love for Joyce, could not as a matter of principle give her special privileges over other children, could not withdraw her from the life of Bermondsey. They regarded this as the supreme test of the sincerity of their decision to turn their backs upon lives of comfort and to identify themselves with the people of Bermondsey. If they withheld their child, if they kept her apart from the children of the men and women among whom they lived, if they sent her away to enjoy opportunities denied to the Bermondsey children, they felt they would be maintaining the very class privilege which they had pledged themselves to destroy and would build a wall between themselves and the people about them. (pp. 29–30)

So Joyce played with local children and attended Keeton Road School. Then in June 1910, Alfred and Ada suffered their most terrible tragedy. Joyce, aged eight, died of scarlet fever. They were devastated. Thereafter they daily decorated Joyce's portraits with flowers or ivy. Their Christian faith, their call to Bermondsey, were tested to the full. They survived, had no more children and expressed their love towards the children of Bermondsey.

One result of Joyce's death was to give Alfred an even greater determination to save the lives of those citizens subject to material disadvantages. His favourite text, not only while preaching in churches but also at political meetings, became 'I am come that they might have life, and that they might have it more abundantly' (John 10.10, Authorized Version). As never before, the Salters perceived that improvements to the health of Bermondsey people depended not just upon skilled doctors but even more on better social conditions. These included decent housing, minimum wages and healthy food. In 1913, they participated in the formation of a co-operative to bake and sell cheap, healthy bread. With Ada as its chairperson, it expanded rapidly and by the 1920s had over 100 employees and sold 75,000 loaves a week, It demonstrated that goods could be provided efficiently with profits shared fairly amongst participants.

Local Politics

Improving social conditions, lessening the gap between Bermondsey and Belgravia, required political action. As early as 1903, Alfred was elected to the borough council for 'the Progressives' which were a part of the Liberal party. But he and Ada were increasingly drawn to socialism which they regarded as more in keeping with Christian doctrine. Alfred was also influenced by his friendship with Charlie Ammon, a sorter in the post office, an active Methodist, and a keen trade unionist. The Liberals were the dominant party and Alfred was being mooted as its next MP. To leave it for the weak socialist movement seemed political suicide. Yet in 1908, Alfred and Ada resigned from the Liberals and went to the inaugural meeting where fourteen members founded the Independent Labour Party in Bermondsey.

The fourteen members were mainly Christians. Their objective, as Brockway puts it, was 'to spread among the people the spirit of fellowship, service and equality' (p. 33). They soon enlisted a following and in 1910 gained an electoral success when Ada won a seat on the Bermondsey Council and so became its first woman councillor. Later others were added, including Alfred, and in

1922 the Labour party won control with Ada as its first mayor. She was the first woman Labour mayor in Britain, with Alfred delighted to offer his services as 'mayoress'. As a Christian and Quaker, Ada declined the pomp of mayoral robes and did away with the formal read prayers which opened council meetings. Instead, she invited members to a time of meditation before the start of proceedings.

The Bermondsey council then set about an expected programme of social reforms. But, unexpectedly, under Ada's guidance, one of its first steps was the establishment of a Beautification Committee. Bermondsey was lacking in trees, flowers and open spaces. With plants and bulbs often taken from Fairby Grange, thousands were planted in the streets. Residents were inspired to cultivate their small gardens or to install window boxes. The flowering of Bermondsey won national praise from the press. Even more importantly, the council set about providing better housing, which Alfred had long argued was essential for better health. Slum property was demolished and council dwellings constructed – although never in sufficient numbers – with indoor toilets, baths and more space.

The Salters' influence was also seen in encouragement of the use of tuberculin-tested milk to prevent TB, the establishment of the first municipal solarium to treat TB, the founding of five infant welfare clinics, and the construction of public baths. It was not just the Salters and they were always insistent on acknowledging the vital contribution of a united team of councillors and officials. Alfred declared, 'We are co-operators in a common purpose. We are trying to make Bermondsey a better and happier place' (pp. 107–8). Their efforts had some success most notably in a fall in the infant mortality rate from 102 deaths per 1,000 infants in 1922 to sixty-seven in 1927, and a drop in the overall mortality rate from 16.7 to 12.9 in the same period. Despite predictions to the contrary, rates did not rise. Efficient administration and preventative policies had paid off.

Member of Parliament

Ada become not only mayor of Bermondsey but also a long-serving and prominent elected member of the London County Council. Meanwhile, Alfred had entered Parliament. Bottom of the poll in 1909, he was elected as member for West Bermondsey in 1922 at the age of forty-nine. His success was short-lived for the Commons was dissolved the following year and he lost the seat. He was an enthusiastic total abstainer and his advocacy of prohibition did not go down well with the working-class electorate. But in 1924 another general election saw him re-elected. In the following years, he identified strongly with striking miners to whom he gave the whole of his parliamentary salary. He was re-elected in 1929 when the Labour party, under Ramsay MacDonald, ran a minority government. Alfred had been tipped as a possible Minister of Health but the pressure of years of continual work now showed in heart strain. He had to rest and then resigned his medical practice and his seat on the council in order to concentrate on Parliament where he had hopes of major reforms despite Britain's economic problems. To his dismay, MacDonald dissolved the Commons in 1931, deserted Labour, and in the ensuing election headed a National party against the Labour party. The latter was overwhelmed and reduced to fifty-two seats. Salter hung on by ninety-one votes.

From 1931 to 1935, the Labour party was led and inspired by Salter's friend, George Lansbury, another politician whose socialism was grounded in Christianity. Alfred's parliamentary contribution had been a disappointment, but now he blossomed leading the opposition in several important debates. His grasp of statistics enabled him to demonstrate how the government's food policies were endangering the health of those on low incomes. He also took up the plight of young offenders and vividly described the circumstances of unemployed sixteen- to twenty-five-year-olds who received no unemployment benefit, who did not want to be a burden to their parents, who were condemned by sections of the press as loafers, and who sometimes resorted to crime. In a speech which could have been made today, Salter argued that the real solution was not longer jail sentences but constructive employment for the young.

Opposition

It should not be thought that the Salters were saints who enjoyed the praise of all around them. They were too puritanical for some, especially Alfred with his outspoken condemnation of smoking and drinking. However, it must be added that both were joyous spirits with Alfred full of loud jokes and cracks and Ada with a consistent quality of peace. Further, as Alfred's biographer admits, 'Salter's own personality did not always make for harmony. He was so confident in his decisions that he was apt to be impatient of criticism and he made such high demands of service and conduct that he tended to be intolerant of those who fell short of his standards' (p. 79). His medical partners sometimes tired of the pace and could be irritated when they were expected to provide cover when he was away at political meetings. Again, Alfred could be scathing towards those who commuted into Bermondsey, who wanted to take its salaries but not live there.

Generally, however, Ada and Alfred had widespread respect and backing in Bermondsey along with many close friends. To them, the main opposition was outside. From the political left, Alfred was criticized by the Communist party for being a compromiser with capitalism and it put up candidates against him. From the political right, some of the health reforms he inspired were dismissed by the national press as waste on the rates, with the new public bathing facilities caricatured as expensive luxuries. More seriously, central government sometimes thwarted local intent. The Bermondsey Council introduced a minimum wage for its own workers at a level which Alfred calculated should be £3.7s.6d a week. The government threatened to surcharge the councillors and to imprison them if they did not withdraw. This did not stop them but, when it introduced a bill to unseat such councillors and to make them ineligible for five years, there was no point in holding out.

The most crushing blow to the Salters, however, was the outbreak of the Second World War. They were lifelong pacifists and Alfred had accompanied George Lansbury – after he lost the leadership of the Labour party over the same issue – on tours against rearmament and aggressive policies. He predicted that war would slay multitudes and destroy whole communities – and so it did in Bermondsey. The Salters, now elderly, refused to be evacuated from Storks Road but were forced to do so by bomb damage. Ada died in 1942 but at least Alfred survived until 1945 and saw the end of the war. When a new Labour government was elected, it was mooted that he should go to the House of Lords. Alfred dismissed the suggestion with contempt. In his last message to friends, he wrote,

> I have tried to fulfil the task which God entrusted to me. I have loved and served the common people and have lived among

them. I have worked unceasingly to bring about a new state of society where all men and women shall be free and equal, where there shall be no poverty or unemployment, where no man shall exploit or dominate his fellow-men, where the cruelty and sorrow of the present system shall be swept away for ever. (p. 241)

Jim Wallis

Jim Wallis was born in 1948 into a devout Plymouth Brethren family in Detroit, USA. He dates his conversion at the age of six and this event, his baptism and acceptance into church member-ship, delighted his family and friends. In his teens, Jim began asking questions about the plight of black people and ventured into the inner city where, as he explains in his autobiography, 'The first thing I discovered, to my great surprise, was that there were black Plymouth Brethren assemblies in Detroit. They were just like my church in most ways, right down to the same dreadful hymnbook, and I wondered why I had never been told about them' (1983, p. 33). Jim initiated a discussion in his church but the response of one elder – that his grandparents had worked their way out of poverty and the blacks should do the same – was typical. They appeared unaware of the social and economic injustices of America.

Alienation from the Church

Wallis' alienation from the Church was completed at Michigan State University where he threw himself into the 'End the Vietnam War' movement. Arrested many times, he argued that the experience of arrest 'fundamentally transforms one's self-consciousness .... To be counted as criminals for the sake of political conscience is the beginning of a taste of what for years has been the experience of poor, black, and Third-World people' (p. 51). Amidst all these campaigns to bring peace, Wallis observed that most evangelical students played no part and con-centrated on trying to convert individuals.

Having rejected the Church, Wallis then became disillusioned with radical student politics. Once the excitement and publicity were over, many students slipped away. They dumped the revolu-tionary struggles for their career struggles. A number became

prosperous academics and Wallis wryly commented, 'For them
the revolution didn't come, but tenure did' (p. 67). Simultaneously, he found no satisfaction in Marxism whose followers,
he perceived, were concerned to manipulate the poor for their
own ends.

The Way Back

Wallis shed the Church and student politics but he wrote, 'I could
never quite get shed of Jesus . . . and at this critical point in my
life he resurfaced to lead me back to himself' (p. 68). He turned
back to the Bible and discovered in Jesus the teaching that
undermined the prevailing values of the world. He wrote, 'I was
deeply struck by a God who had taken up residence among the
poor, the oppressed, the outcasts. How much we love Jesus . . . is
determined by how much we serve those who are at the bottom
of society' (p. 71).

Jim Wallis then enrolled at an evangelical theological college
where his radical Christianity soon disturbed traditionalists. He
found some kindred spirits and, in 1971, they launched a magazine, *The Post-American*, so called because it sought to break free
from the dominant American connection between conservative
theology and conservative politics. It argued that biblical Christianity led to an identification with poor people. Later the title
was changed to *Sojourners* to reflect the biblical teaching of a people who were fully engaged in the world but whose values were
drawn from the kingdom of God. The magazine gained a high
circulation and became a powerful voice throughout America.

The students also accepted the idea of community and so lived
with each other. The initial group became too concerned with
debating its ideal structure, began to neglect love and to foster
rivalries. They also had to learn that it was not just the affluent
who had idols: the radicals could boast about their involvement
with the poor, which was as damaging as pride in possessions.
Some left but the remainder discovered that they had to rely upon
God not on their own abilities, had to learn to forgive and love
each other.

Sojourners

After leaving college in 1975, eighteen adults and two babies
moved into two houses in downtown Washington DC. These

Sojourners grew to forty with their community having three main characteristics. One was economic simplicity: they rejected over-consumption and consumerism, lived modestly and shared goods equally. The second was worship: praise, prayer, Bible study, communion, put God at the centre. The third was servanthood: a commitment to being with and on the side of poor people. Overall, Wallis summed up by stating, 'we see our role as simply calling people to faith, to a recovery of our commitment to Jesus Christ. The renewal of faith is finally the only thing with the strength to resist the economic and political powers, and to provide an adequate spiritual foundation for a more just way to live' (p. 99).

The Sojourners wanted to serve the poor in a society in which, as Wallis put it, 'the official neglect of the poor is sanctioned and even justified in the name of sound fiscal policy. The poor are always made to pay for the sins of the rest of society. Always' (p. 109). They befriended local, mainly black, families, started after-school clubs, introduced tutoring schemes to encourage their educational progress. Tenants facing eviction were represented and stimulus given to the formation of tenants' associations which sometimes withheld rent to persuade landlords to carry out repairs. More fundamentally, other tenants combined to purchase their properties and to run them as co-operatives.

This is not to pretend there were no failures. Wallis sadly points to families whom he has known for years whose children are now on drugs. A locally controlled day care centre collapsed when growing unemployment meant parents could no longer pay its fees. One group of tenants bought out their landlord only to find that an expected government grant for refurbishment was not forthcoming. But the Sojourners survived, were accepted by residents, and still flourish today.

The Soul of Politics

Wallis still lives in the same community, where, as he said to the present writer, 'we work with kids who go to bed to the sound of gunfire every single night, 20 blocks from the White House, and for me its a spiritual discipline to be rooted in that reality and in the experience of the people I write about' (B. Holman, 1995). In 1995, Jim Wallis toured Britain to publicize his book *The Soul of Politics*. In it, he still reveals the justified anger at society's inequalities which drove him into action. He calls Washington DC 'A tale of two cities' and contrasts the plight of the homeless with some of the most expensive housing in the USA; the infant mortality rates of the poor reaching Third World proportions with the large number of estate agents and lawyers for the rich; the 60 per cent unemployment amongst black young people with the professional couples with two huge incomes; the hungry with a meeting at the Sheraton Hotel where politicians were 'talking about feeding the hungry, while they dined on poached fillet of salmon with saffron cream' (1995, p. 61).

Wallis still proclaims biblical Christianity. He said, 'I am unapologetic about my faith in Jesus Christ' but he respects other faiths, adding, 'I often find myself in jail, and I run into Muslims there who are doing tremendous work' (B. Holman, 1995). He has recently worked alongside Muslims in gathering together 164 gang leaders in an effort to stop violence. More generally, he acknowledges that society has to be changed by politics but that this requires politics to be transformed. He stated,

> Both of the economic paradigms (communist and capitalist) have failed. They've failed the poor, the earth, and the human heart. Now, only one of them has admitted its failure; the other proclaims its victory. I laugh when I hear the victorious pronouncement of corporate capitalism. From where I look at it, I see the devastation of neighbourhoods where the only market economy is crack cocaine and MacDonald's. There are no jobs. (B. Holman, 1995)

He has little confidence in present political parties, stating that 'Liberalism is unable to articulate or demonstrate the kind of moral values that must undergird any serious movement of social transformation . . . . Conservatism still denies the reality of structural injustice and social oppression' (1995, p. xii).

Wallis believes change is possible and points to what has happened in South Africa. He does not consider it is realistic to detail an economic blueprint for the future but he does insist that values can be articulated and that any change must be achieved in conjunction with those at the bottom of society. He calls for community politics based on local action which could be acceptable to both left and right. These solutions and their common values could then be part of a bottom-up movement to reshape national politics. He wants the Church to contribute by proclaiming the whole gospel and by investing its resources in the inner cities. He wants Christians to put biblical principles into practice by the way they live their daily lives.

Bron Soan

Born in the Midlands in 1935, Bronwyn Soan commenced early a somewhat nomadic form of life. Her parents were strong Christians and socialists whose faith endured the death, from TB, of their two-year-old son. Mr Soan was a low-paid Baptist minister in Coventry but, on the outbreak of war in 1939, he resigned his position in order to shed any ministerial protection while he argued his case as a conscientious objector. A tribunal accepted his case and, before long, the Soans joined a co-operative farming venture in which all things were held in common. They then returned to Coventry just before the massive bombing of that city. The Soans – parents and two daughters – were staying in a hostel into which moved some evacuees and bomb victims. Being pacifists they took some verbal abuse from the victims of the war but they stuck to their beliefs. In 1942, they moved again to a dilapidated cottage in Wales – no electricity, no toilets, no running water – which cost £5 a year. In time, by dint of hard work and borrowing, Mr and Mrs Soan managed to buy their own farm for £600.

Socialist and Agnostic

The war over, Bron left school at fifteen to seek work in Swansea. She was sacked from her first job because of her militant communism and efforts to recruit staff to the cause. Soon after she left communism and joined the Young Socialists. She had continued to attend a Baptist church but soon after lost her faith and, as a student nurse, she preferred pubs to church. By her early twenties, Bron was a midwife in London. She then spent four years in the USA and Canada where she would introduce herself with, 'Hello, I'm Bron and I'm a socialist and agnostic.'

Following a period in Israel, Bron decided to switch to social work and obtained a place on a child care officers' course at the Stevenage College of Further Education. I was a young lecturer at the college and so, for the first time, met the intelligent, articulate, argumentative and outspoken Bron. She made no secret of her radicalism and her dislike of Christianity.

Still Searching

As a child care officer in local authority Children's Departments, Bron's abilities were soon recognized, she was promoted into posts of responsibility. Following changes in the organization of the personal social services, she joined the new Glasgow Social Work Department as a team leader in 1968. Outside work, she was attracted to the Gorbals Group and its leader, the Revd Geoff Shaw. Geoff was a Church of Scotland minister who later became a councillor and leader of the new Strathclyde Region. But, as his biographer, Ron Ferguson puts it, 'perhaps his greatest and most disturbing gift to us is the haunting symbol of a battered, ever-open door at 74, Cleland Street, Gorbals' (1979, preface). A Christian who lived amongst poor people and who was involved in Labour party politics had great appeal for Bron and she sometimes ventured into the Group's religious gatherings. Bron explained to me in an interview in 1996,

> I was still agnostic and when Geoff passed the bread and wine I just handed it to the next person. Yet it was meaningful to me and as I sat and heard the traffic outside and the Gorbals noises I thought, 'This is what Christianity should be about.' I continued to argue with Geoff just as I used to argue with you and Annette and challenge you, 'Come on, convince me.' I recall going to the Gorbals Daffodil Fair where I had my handwriting read and two years running the woman wrote down, 'You are a deeply religious person.' I went around showing it to all my friends and laughing hilariously – but I felt a bit uncomfortable.

Eventually Bron decided to return south to be near her ailing parents. She applied for a post as a principal officer in a Social Services Department and, at the interview, declared, 'As a socialist and an agnostic I think it is immoral that you should be paying £8,000 a year salary for this job.' She still got the post. Bron continued, 'I was still searching. I would go to the library and pick out books from each section. I was still looking for heroes and heroines. Keir Hardie was one. I was also looking for a partner and got very disappointed. I joined Amnesty International and still support it.'

At the age of forty-two, Bron took an unofficial sabbatical. She stayed with her parents, worked as a volunteer with OXFAM and did stints in children's homes. Then she started attending the

Anglican church in Hay-on-Wye in order to be near a man she fancied – only to find out that he was a homosexual. Bron explained,

> I said to myself, 'I must not come here just because of him.' I discovered something else. I started to pray in a very naive and straightforward way saying, 'OK, God, I came here because of this man, nevertheless I would like to find you.' And I did. I got friendly with the vicar who lent me books and eventually I was baptized and confirmed. I felt comfortable. I belonged. Then things fell apart. I had to have an operation which meant I could not have kids, which was the hardest thing of my life. Next I got breast cancer. I remember a Christian friend saying, 'The Lord is testing you.' I replied, 'I don't think the Lord gives cancer but hopefully he will help me cope with it.' In hospital the lump was nipped out. Others died. I found I was able to care for other patients. Before I had been quite a competent nurse but now, being a Christian, I discovered that I did it with extra love.

El Salvador

Thereafter Bron went back to nursing for several years. She was eager to share her Christian faith and wore a cross as a means of introduction. During this time, her eventful life took another turn when she read about indigenous people being massacred in El Salvador. She joined Human Rights for Central America, taught herself Spanish, and made her way to El Salvador, initially for a month. Thereafter, her lifestyle became that of working for a few months in Britain as a nurse or social worker in order both to raise money for her new friends and also to afford to travel and stay there each year. So far she has been eleven times. She said,

> I lived with Catholic nuns. I read liberation theology and found this was what I understood – in a nutshell it is liberation from sin – and poverty is a sin. There was war all the time. I so admired the people there. I was bombed with them, machine-gunned with them, we used the same overflowing toilet, we shared the same bowls of food. I was humbled. Just as in Glasgow, the poor shared with the poor. There were no doctors so I took on that role. We lived in the mountains, very isolated. I identified with them and decided to become a Catholic and was received into the church in front of all the people. It was

lovely, the doors are open in the church, dogs wander in and scratch themselves, kids run up and down and sit on your lap – and this is how it should be. I walked up the aisle and the guy who was confirming me asked me how I came to their religion. I replied that it was thanks to everyone there, including the children. It meant a lot to them, and it certainly did to me.

When I came back to Britain, I received instruction from a traditional priest and was confirmed at Hay-on-Wye. I have been dedicated once, baptized twice, confirmed three times. So I am a Christian, but not for these reasons, because Christianity is about how you live. I sometimes think how surprising it is that I am a Christian. Twice it really has come home to me. Once in El Salvador the bombing was very close and I thought, 'This is it.' I just prayed, 'Help me comport myself as a Christian. I commit myself to you, Lord.'

Afterwards, I felt, 'Crumbs, I really do believe.' The other time, I was feeling lonely and thought, 'I wish I hadn't been born.' Immediately, I had another thought. 'But I would not have known the love of God.' Again it came to me, 'You are a Christian.'

Still Serving

In between her trips abroad, Bron worked mainly as a nurse. She sent two-thirds of her earnings to El Salvador. Now that she has reached the age of sixty she has officially retired. She continues to live frugally, buying most of her clothes from charity shops. Sometimes she takes a short-term job, gives all the salary to El Salvador and Amnesty International, and survives on her pension. She said, 'As a socialist, I gave 10 per cent of my salary; as a Christian – where do you stop? They are God's people so you give everything.'

In terms of activity, Bron is anything but retired. She became aware of families in Britain who do not get holidays, who cannot afford the private leisure which is available to the affluent. She explained, 'I feel so angry about the injustices, the inequalities in society. It is so immoral.' So at the age of sixty-one, Bron purchased a run-down cottage by a Scottish loch and opened it to families from Glasgow. She has taken some from Easterhouse where I live.

In the autumn of 1996, Bron had to return temporarily to Herefordshire to be with her sister whose husband had suddenly died. She plans to come back to Scotland in 1997. She is also planning another trip to her beloved El Salvador. As she puts it, 'I feel most at home with the church in El Salvador. They worship as they live. You serve God wherever you are. You serve each other. I just want to serve. That sounds so flaming pious but it is a privilege to serve and that is all I ask.'

Common Features

Ada and Alfred Salter died in England over fifty years ago. Jim Wallis lives in the USA. Bron Soan is in active retirement in Scotland. They are different kinds of people, from different generations, from different countries. Yet their lives have at least three features in common.

God First

Jim Wallis does not align himself with any political party although he is active in the peace movement. It is clear from what he writes and from what is written about him that his primary allegiance is not to a secular organization but to God. His obedience brought him into some heart-breaking differences with his parents, with public authorities, and indeed, took him to prison.

The Salters, like their friend George Lansbury, were political activists who believed that a Christian society, characterized by equality, was more likely to be promoted through the Labour party than any other. They therefore devoted much of their time to politics. But God came even before the party. It was put to Alfred that his outspoken opposition to alcohol was a vote-loser and might even keep him from becoming a government minister. He retorted, 'I would bow my knee to no one except my Maker' (Brockway, p. 118). He and Ada accepted that Jesus Christ had forbidden violence and they held on to their views even when pacifism became unacceptable within the Labour party. Again, Alfred criticized the institutions of the monarchy and the House of Lords, although to do so was to invite the press to portray him as an extremist who should not be in Parliament. He stuck to his position because he believed that these inherited positions were out of keeping with Christian beliefs in democracy and equality.

Bron Soan has reached pensionable age with little money and few possessions because she has been prepared to follow the lifestyle of Jesus Christ. These Christians have put obedience to God before political parties, status, power, popularity and comfort. They have practised equality because it is a part of their obedience to God.

Location

The Salters, Jim Wallis and Bron Soan could have lived almost anywhere. Ada and Alfred loved the countryside and were sometimes tempted to dwell there. Jim Wallis could take a ministerial post in a large, rich church. Bron Soan, a talented social worker, could have climbed to the top of that profession and commuted in from the suburbs. Instead, the Salters stayed in Bermondsey, Jim Wallis is in downtown Washington, Bron Soan spent much of her time in the front line in El Salvador. It is not being argued that all Christians have to vacate their comfortable surroundings and immediately descend upon the areas of social deprivation. However, there is little doubt that those who do reside in such places have a significant role in promoting equality. They are alongside those in greatest social need and this means:

- that barriers between different sections of society are removed;
- that more money is spent in under-resourced, local economies;
- that they can work in mutuality with longer-standing residents to strengthen neighbourhood institutions such as schools, shops, voluntary bodies;
- that they can co-operate with those who have low incomes to articulate the reforms that are required to bring about a more equal society.

Stickability

It is not unusual for young people, with good intentions, to move into a deprived area only to leave after a year or so. Their departure may follow having their car vandalized or their flat raided or because they believe that outside schools would be better for their children. The short-stay can do harm for local residents who may conclude that, despite all their radical words, they had come just to gather material for a research project or to put on their CV that they had lived in a deprived zone. In short, the residents can feel used. The Salters, Jim Wallis, Bron Soan gave themselves long-term. It is over time that trust is developed. It is over the years that the incomers really make the locality their home, make enduring friendships, identify with, and truly become a part of local activities.

These three features are common to three examples of people who live out equality. Lack of space prohibits detailing the lives of others. I have concentrated on instances of Christians because this is a book which strives to make the connection between Christianity and equality. But it is not just Christians. Others are also committed to equality and demonstrate it in the quality of their living. They do so by refusing to reinforce inequality by taking the huge salaries and excessive wealth which would take them into the top section of the equality–inequality league and they do so by choosing to co-operate with those who are at the bottom end. In short, they practise the fairer sharing of material resources within a context of mutual relationships. This is the path to equality.

Influencing Others

I do not wish to give the impression that only those who originate outside of the inner cities and council estates can lead the progress along this path. Far from it. George Lansbury is an example of an East Ender who fought inequality by refusing to move away from Bow Road, by organizing and activating those he had known from childhood. But the fact is that many Christians, such as Jim Wallis, do start life in the more affluent suburbs. For them, the first step may be to relocate but they must do so, as in the case of Wallis, in the spirit of servanthood. Then together, those from outside and those long-standing residents from inside can practise the values, the mutuality, the action, the proclamation, the lifestyles, which are an expression of equality. Hopefully they will succeed in running local organizations, such as food co-ops and credit unions, where service for all comes before personal gain, where employees have small differentials in their salaries.

Hopefully, they will succeed in convincing government that structural reforms are required. But even if these outcomes do not occur in the short-term, it is likely that those who live equality will attract others to the cause. Fenner Brockway, concluded his biography of Alfred Salter by stating, 'The example of his life, his heroic fidelity to principle, his utter self-giving to his ideals, lit an inspiration which endures. Thousands of men and women learned to have a new faith in humanity because they saw in him the promise of what the good life might be' (p. 242).

Jim Wallis' lifestyle encouraged others to follow in his direction. Throughout this book I have made a number of references to George Lansbury, whose capacity to uphold the values of equality by personal conduct made a powerful impression on me. A contemporary wrote about him, 'We younger men will never be able to say what we owe to George Lansbury from the example he has set us all, of a consistent self-sacrificing life, of a constant and fearless witness to Jesus Christ' (B. Holman, 1990, p. 172).

It will be countered that the Salters, Wallis, Lansbury were well-known figures and could be expected to exert more influence than those who are not in the news. Maybe, but Bron Soan is not a national figure. I am encouraged and strengthened by her life which is far better than my own. I know too that ordinary residents of Easterhouse, who have come into contact with her, have been moved by the simplicity of her lifestyle, by her insistence on sharing, and by the application of her faith. Interestingly, after visiting her cottage, some Easterhouse residents then sought and got her a second-hand washing machine. They appreciate Bron all the more because they have been able to help her – mutuality. Most of us will not be famous but we can all attempt to put our principles into practice and, in so doing, may draw others into the pursuit of equality.

Christians should want other people to enter into an individual relationship with God simply because they believe that God made them for this purpose. It follows that Christians should, by word and deed, encourage them to do so. Christians should also seek an end to the vast inequalities of Britain because – if I understand the Bible correctly – God has created all people equal in his sight and equal in regard to each other. All should have similar access to the resources of the world and all should be in relationships of mutuality towards fellow creatures.

I am not suggesting that the churches and Christians can achieve the equal society on their own. Numerically, church membership may be shrinking. None the less, the Church still has a voice in Britain. Locally churches are often better attended than party political meetings, and as indicated above, the individual influence of Christians can be effective. Christians can pursue equality by joining political parties and pressing them to give priority to structural reforms. They can encourage their churches to practise and proclaim equality. They can participate in neighbourhood groups. Perhaps, above all, their sincerity will be reflected in the quality of their day-to-day lives and this may encourage others to join them. But however they express the case for equality, one result is for sure – they will have to counter the objections of the opposition, of those who want to uphold inequality.

6

◦◦━◦◦

Objections to Equality

Years ago, as a young lecturer, I chaired a joint staff–student seminar on poverty. It was the radical 1960s and we Social Science staff felt rather smug: we were publishing books about poverty, telling the Labour government how to improve its legislation, and now we were demonstrating our solidarity with students by opening up our monthly seminar to them. Some of the students were associated with the Claimants' Union, a new collective made up of recipients of Social Security. My smugness began to fade as one student criticized academics who used the poor to make good livings from lecturing and writing books about the socially deprived.

Then another student put forward arguments for equality of incomes. It was more than the professor could stand. He was for higher welfare benefits, he gave lectures on whether Labour's pension proposals would improve the standards of elderly people, he was a member of the Child Poverty Action Group – but equality! 'Do you mean,' he asked the student, 'that I should be paid the same as a shop assistant?' He then launched forth with a list of objections to equality. Even in those heady years, the most trendy of poverty campaigners could suddenly find themselves defending inequality if fingers were pointed at them.

The 1990s are certainly not years of radicalism. The objections to equality are expressed even more widely and strongly. In this chapter, I try to set out some of these criticisms and then to counter them. In defending equality, I must object to the objectors.

The Anti-Levellers

A frequent objection to the case for equality is that it will bring all people to the same level. The levellers – as egalitarians are

116

sometimes called – will produce a drab uniformity in which all people are the same dull robots. Further, the levelling off of incomes will take away any incentive to work.

Christian Precedents

Levelling down should not be dismissed so easily. Jesus himself levelled down for 'though he was rich, yet for our sake he became poor, so that by his poverty you might become rich' (2 Corinthians 8.9). The Son of God set aside the location of heaven and the worship of angels to dwell with ordinary men and women. Now that is levelling down. I think the primary meaning of this passage is that Jesus came down to the level of people like us so that we might have a full knowledge of him. None the less, in entering this world Jesus did choose to level down in terms of income, wealth and lifestyle.

The early Church quickly got the message, 'All the believers agreed to hold everything in common; they began to sell their property and possessions and distribute to everyone according to his need' (Acts 2.44–5). Obviously, some members levelled down so that others could level up. Later, the Gentile churches gave money in order to support the poorer church in Jerusalem.

The practice of levelling down is in line with Christian example. And today there should be no objection to levelling down if it means that the disadvantages of others are removed. The levellers will still have sufficient to live comfortably while they will also have the satisfaction of knowing that their mutuality has 'made rich' those who were poor. The end result is likely to be a more level, and hence a more, united society.

Dull Uniformity?

What of the claim of the Anti-Levellers that levelling down will bring about a dull and drab uniformity? My observation is that, at present, the people at the top are not immune from uniformity. City financiers wear similar suits, go to similar clubs where they talk in similar accents about the same subject – money. If they did level down they might find more variety and enrichment by mixing with people from different localities and backgrounds and with different interests. Margaret Drabble – drawing upon the writings of the egalitarian Bernard Shaw, whom nobody could call drab – argues that levelling would mean the reverse of uniformity.

If the incomes of the bottom 30 per cent of the population were increased, then more talents would flourish and more choices be open to those who now live restricted lives. She amusingly takes the example of oysters which were much enjoyed by the poor in Dickens' day but are now beyond their pockets. If a levelling out meant that they could again exercise this choice,

> It would not condemn the dons of Oxford and Cambridge to a diet of whelks and chip butties. It would offer real choice, not the illusion of choice. Nor would it condemn us all to living in council blocks with second hand Utility furniture and sagging mattresses and three ducks on the wall and foam-filled, lethal, cheap three-piece suites. No, we would be able to choose better furniture, more various styles of architecture, less lethal three-piece suites. (1988, p. 5)

Economic Motivation

The most common argument of the Anti-Levellers is that inequality is necessary as an economic motivation, that people will only work hard at the prospect of more and more financial reward. William Letwin, in his well-known essay 'The Case Against Equality' asserts that the removal of inequality 'is certain to destroy or diminish most people's incentives to work, so reducing the prosperity of each and all' (M. Desai, ed., 1995, pp. 91–2). Graham Dawson adds that 'the lack of such an incentive will certainly inhibit some workers and entrepreneurs from wealth creation and so further depress the standards of living of the worse off' (D. Anderson, ed., 1984, p. 18). The claim, then, is that inequality not only provides the motivation to work, it also enriches the whole of society by creating more wealth.

The above argument ignores the fact that much wealth in Britain is not earned by hard work but by inheritance. As Sidney and Beatrice Webb put it in the language of their time, 'under the reign of capitalism, those who own the most, not those who work the most, get, in fact, the largest incomes; and those who own the least get, in fact, the smallest incomes, however hard they work' (M. Desai, ed., p. 174). But ignoring unearned income, the claim that large differences in rewards are necessary to make people work hard does not stand up to examination. It is true that, amongst the very affluent, the drive to obtain yet more is a powerful one. But the desire to work, to be in paid employment, is very strong throughout our society irrespective of size of income. Indeed, reviewing research surveys, Anthony Heath reveals that it is high amongst all groupings – even those on welfare benefits (D. Smith, ed., 1992, chapter 3).

I was brought up during the War when millions of workers toiled for long hours in difficult conditions. Obtaining high pay was not a primary factor because they were united in a common purpose that was not economic. Of course, war was an exceptional circumstance. But, as shown in the last chapter, people will work hard for moderate but sufficient wages if committed to certain values. Human beings are more than economic animals driven solely by material gain. Work provides outlets for skills, friendships, a sense of achievement. The desire to be in employment is deeply held in our society and does not have to be stimulated by the possibility of very high financial rewards. In short, people will work in a more level society if the values they hold are in accord with mutuality, if they are driven by a sense of mutual obligation.

Furthermore, the argument that a very unequal society is necessary to produce a prosperous nation, to keep people in employment, and indeed, to enrich the whole of society, is not borne out by personal experience nor by academic studies. During the last twenty or so years, Britain has become a more uneven society: wage differences are huge; the government has increasingly urged people to work harder to earn more and has frequently condemned and criticized the unemployed. I live in the east end of Glasgow and know that most people want to work. Yet, as Professor Michael Pacione shows, during the years in which inequality has been held up as a virtue, poverty and unemployment have worsened. In Easterhouse, the male unemployment rate actually increased from 35.1 per cent in 1981 to 44.8 per cent in 1991 (1995, p. 234).

It is not sufficient just to cite the area where I dwell. Two studies published in 1996 show the same internationally. The United Nations issued its *Human Development Report* which drew much comment from financial journalists. Victor Keegan stated that 'it concludes that the assumption of the 1980s and early 1990s – that more equal distribution of incomes would destroy incentives and that the rich needed special encouragement to save and invest – have proved false' (1996). Further, the Organisation for Economic Co-operation and Development – which had previously been an advocate of a deregulated market and low wages – has concluded that inequality is an economic blight and that those countries which have become more level in their income distribution have been the more economically successful.

The reasons appear to be twofold. First, the emphasis on making quick and large profits has led to financiers seeking short-term gains which involves laying off staff and a failing to invest in the long-term needs of industry, such as in new machinery. Consequently, unemployment rises and, with it, poverty and public expenditure on unemployment pay, while simultaneously, industry, particularly manufacturing industry, grows weaker in comparison with other countries. Second, in the more equal countries, where greater value is placed upon all people, more public investment is made in education and training. Edward Balls, drawing upon the OECD report writes, 'the east Asian countries highlight the close relationship between equality, skills and growth . . . the combination of greater income equality and very high school-enrolment rates explains about 90 per cent of the higher growth achieved' (1996).

To conclude, levelling down is not an evil. It certainly does not lead to drabness and dullness. Socially it can make for a more integrated, less fragmented society. Economically, it benefits the whole community for it can lead to greater prosperity for all – although shared out more fairly – and lower unemployment.

The Economic Right

Probably the most ferocious critics of the concept and practice of equality are from what may be called the Economic Right. Already they have been referred to as the New Right in that their influence was strongest when Margaret Thatcher, as Prime Minister, was rejecting as 'soft' the beliefs of former right wing governments, particularly that led by Ted Heath. But the Economic Right traces its ideas back to Adam Smith and more recently to Friedrich Hayek whose powerful book *The Road to Serfdom* was so influential in the 1940s and 1950s (1944). Some New Right leaders have a harsh and uncaring edge, particularly in regard to vulnerable groups such as lone mothers and the homeless. But not all. In *The Kindness that Kills* some prominent right wing members, some of whom are also Christians, express their views. Professor Brian Griffiths, for example, draws upon the Bible to acknowledge that 'The case for an anti-poverty policy is certainly a strong one' (D. Anderson, ed., 1984, p. 106). None the less they are opposed to equality.

Wealth Creation

One objection made by the Economic Right is that egalitarians ignore the importance of the creation of wealth. Graham Dawson even says that they express the ancient 'heresy of Manicheism, which is the belief that matter is evil, from which it follows that any involvement with the material world, including the extraction of its natural resources and their manufacture into material goods, is corrupting' (p. 13). It may be true that Christian egalitarians have not contributed much to the literature of wealth creation. It is true that Christian egalitarians like myself believe that matter – money, food, consumer goods – can be an evil if it dominates our lives, if it becomes an obsession which mars our relationship with our God and which diminishes our concern for our neighbours. But we certainly do not think that matter is evil in itself. On the contrary, we acknowledge that material resources are a part of God's creation and we want them to be enjoyed and shared as equally as possible. Anyone who participates in a neighbourhood group which issues low credit, has a food co-op for cheap food, makes holidays available at reasonable prices, buys Traidcraft goods in order to encourage groups abroad which are running small businesses and co-ops, will know that material things are regarded as important. But just as important is that they are distributed fairly.

Differences in Income

A strong objection of the Economic Right is to the small differences in income which are inherent in a more equal society. As Brian Griffiths puts it, 'There is no problem in defending the morality of economic inequalities that result from differences in skills, energy, ambition and the freedom to work' (p. 112). Their argument is twofold, namely that workers who do more valuable and important work should receive far higher financial rewards than those who do not; and also that the free market works out its own rewards so if a company decides to pay its chairman £2 million a year and its factory workers £12,000 a year, so be it.

The response that great differences create enormous social disadvantages for those at the bottom need not be repeated here. Barbara Wootton carefully questions the justification for paying one worker fifty times more than another (today it would be a 100 times as much). She points out that one person is unlikely to be fifty times as more intelligent than another. She concludes that it is impossible to quantify the value of work to society. She agrees, for instance, that a doctor does more for health than an ambulance driver but, she adds, the doctor receives years of training at the community's expense and should be expected to make a return. Moreover, many doctors enter their occupation primarily to be of use to others not to become rich.

It might be added that a nursery school teacher does an immensely important job in training young children – indeed recent research suggests that high quality nursery education can prevent many children becoming delinquents with all their social and economic costs to society – yet nursery teachers receive comparatively low wages compared with a Director of Education. The explanation is that the latter carries more responsibility, but is there much greater responsibility than directly shaping the lives of children?

Turning to business, Wootton finds no evidence that 'the highest pay attracts the best men. Would it not be more logical to suppose that it would attract the most acquisitive, that is those who are primarily interested in money?' (1976, p. 4). In short, she sees no justification for huge differences in income.

One of the most significant yet most neglected parables told by Jesus is that of the workers in the vineyard. The owner settled on a fair wage with those who started in the morning and then the same with those who started later. When the early workers grumbled because they had done more, he replied, 'My friend, I am not being unfair to you. You agreed on the usual wage for the day .... Why be jealous because I am generous?' (Matthew 20.13–15). The parable is sometimes interpreted to mean that, at whatever stage we become Christians, we shall all receive the same heavenly reward. This may well be correct but Jesus also used it to explain what his kingdom is like and it is clear that we should be trying to follow the nature of the kingdom on this earth. Central to the parable is a belief, now neglected, that the earth is the Lord's. And not just the earth, he also created human brains, hands and skills. The millionaire who retorts that he made all his money with his own abilities and so can take what he likes is wrong. The Lord made those abilities. He should be thankful that God has so equipped him and be satisfied with a fair income even if it is not much above that of others. The teaching of this parable is that of fairness, indeed equality, in income allocation. The reason is that God is generous and we should be the same in distributing any resources. As explained previously, I am not arguing for exact equality in income for that would be impossible to achieve. I am arguing that there is no justification for the huge differences which emerge from the unfettered market economy. A small ratio of difference will not only remove many of the deprivations of our society, it will also express the spirit of generosity which springs from the principle of mutuality.

Political Regimes

The Economic Right attacks the objective of equality on the grounds that it would entail or lead to an extremist political system. It is hinted that egalitarians are at one with the kind of totalitarian regimes of the former East European republics. William Letwin concludes his polemic by asserting that the achievement of equality will usher in 'tyranny' (M. Desai, ed., p. 136). The Economic Right is correct to attack regimes which suppress democracy and human liberties and, hopefully, they will also aim their attack on those which combine the free market with dictatorship. But the kind of equality of which I have been writing is nothing to do with the former communist inspired states. Martin Luther King was subject to the accusation of being a communist. He responded in a famous sermon in which he clearly made the distinctions between Christianity and communism. He pointed out that under communism, man is made for the state and has no value apart from which he contributes to the state. He continued,

All of this is contrary, not only to the Christian doctrine of God, but also to the Christian estimate of man. Christianity insists that man is an end because he is the child of God, made in God's image. Man is more than a producing animal guided by economic forces; he is a being of spirit, crowned with glory and honour, endowed with the gift of freedom. The ultimate weakness of Communism is that it robs man of that quality which makes him man. (1975, pp. 98–9)

Christians believe that human beings are more important than the state and also more important than the free market. Christian egalitarians hold that the promotion of equality is consistent with the kind of society God wants for his creation and that they should seek to ensure that resources are distributed towards this end. But they also believe that the value of all human beings should be expressed through democratic methods. It follows that the Economic Right should not associate this form of equality with Soviet style states.

The Means to Equality

Next, the Economic Right dislikes the readiness of egalitarians to use the state to promote equality. As explained above, Christian egalitarians are opposed to the state being the master of human beings. Instead, they believe that the public, through democratic means, should use the mechanisms of the state to promote equality. The Economic Right is opposed to equality but they also have a deep suspicion of using state resources, particularly money raised by income tax, even to alleviate poverty. Robert Miller claims that governments lack the knowledge of how to intervene in economic affairs, while Brian Griffiths states that 'by breeding dependence on handouts, the redistribution of wealth through the coercive power of the state can make matters worse' (p. 106). What should be the means of helping the poor? According to the Economic Right, it should be left to the free market.

One of the oddities about the Economic Right is that their objections to state action are most voiced against the poor. The enormous salary increase to MPs made in 1996 puts another £8 million on to public expenditure. Yet the most vehement supporters of this increase were those simultaneously calling for cut backs in state spending. Other critics of state spending have been university professors who, for years, have readily taken ample salaries and research grants from public money. Some have even gone to the House of Lords where, again, they receive excessive allowances from money raised through taxation. Outside of Parliament, there have indeed been cutbacks and the numbers directly employed in the public sector have shrunk by 50 per cent since 1979. But total state expenditure has increased. Part of the explanation is that the expenditure has been shifted towards placing contracts with private firms, hiring private consultants and creating unelected quangos. Apparently, then, the state does possess the knowledge to intervene in economic matters and is justified in using huge amounts of public money.

The market can contribute to economic growth and is a major means of setting prices and distributing goods. The market should have a place in the free society. But it – no more than any other mechanism – should not be exalted as the sole, supreme means of economic growth and distribution. The unregulated market has obvious limitations. The growth it stimulates is often accompanied by massive unemployment and low wages – in short, it is a cause of poverty. It does not distribute its rewards in a fair manner – the financier who manipulates markets may make millions, the worker producing food and goods very little. The market system does not necessarily produce the goods which are most needed – only those which private forces can pay for. Thus it may turn out thousands of four-bedroomed mock Tudor, detached houses for the affluent, but few smaller and cheaper homes for those living in overcrowded squalor. Not least, the market experiences booms and slumps which are not understood. Indeed, knowledge about it is no more advanced than that about state mechanisms.

State intervention either by direct services or by taxation clearly has its dangers. It can lead to inflation and to large bureaucracies. But it must be noted, public, collective action grew precisely because of the failings of the market system. It is the state which has been largely responsible for the development of education and health services. It is the state, through the introduction of Family Allowances, which did much to alleviate child poverty. State services can be conveyed, as with the NHS, in ways which are perfectly acceptable to the public or, as with means-tested services, which impart stigma. However, as already mentioned, there is little evidence that state benefits reduce the desire of most people to be in employment.

Both the free market and state mechanisms are the result of human decision-making. Steps should be taken to ensure that they are not used to damage lives but rather to enhance the quality of life for as many people as possible. Frank Field MP, Will Hutton, John King and Professors David Marquand and John Gray have written an important article which identifies both positive and negative elements in the British free market system. They refute the claim that the market can deal with inequalities and write,

'The claim that the market is self-regulating and no more is false. The market reinforces adverse trends.' In short, under the market, the rich get richer and the poor get poorer. The failures of the market do not lead them to call for its abolition. Instead, they call for a reformed market system, one which encourages firms to move away from giving priority to short-term large profits to directors, top managers and shareholders, to one which builds up the long-term strengths of companies, which invests in machinery and training. This, they feel, is the way to economic prosperity and less unemployment (F. Field, et al., 1996). At the same time, state intervention and services are also needed. State services which, for instance, provide quality care in sickness and old age mean that users do not depend on an ability to pay – equality of care.

Moreover, tax and fiscal policies can lead to a fairer distribution of income and wealth. State policies to boost employment cannot only take workers off the dole, but also can put them in a position where their work and spending contributes to the strong economy and the common good. Will Hutton calculates that a return to full male employment would save £36 billion annually in social security payouts ('A state of decay', 1995). As he puts it, 'The fight against poverty is not merely a moral injunction: the just society begets the sound economy' ('The real price of poverty', 1992).

Interestingly, Hutton is here reviving an argument put forward by Hugh Dalton, later a Chancellor of the Exchequer, in the 1920s. He stated, 'for each individual, marginal economic welfare diminishes as income increases. Then, if a given income is to be distributed among a given number of persons, it is evident that economic welfare will be at a maximum, when all incomes are equal' (M. Desai, ed., p. 139). In other words, Dalton is saying that the more money is shared amongst many individuals, the more it is put to useful ends. For instance, today it is more useful for residents of deprived areas to have extra money to spend on the essentials which can revive the local economy than for it to go to millionaires to spend on yachts or to place in tax havens.

Equality, this book argues, is a Christian aim and it has suggested ways in which Christians might try to persuade others that it is a legitimate aim for all. If public attitudes are influenced by mutuality and there is a widespread desire for greater equality then the public, through its democratic processes, is entitled to advance it through both the market and state intervention.

The Financial Pessimists

An objection made by both those sympathetic to and opposed to equality is that Britain could not afford it. In particular, the financial pessimists claim that any redistribution of incomes would involve higher taxes for many people which would not be acceptable in an already highly taxed nation.

The Tax System

In fact, in terms of income tax Britain is one of the least taxed countries in Europe. Its high earners, including 95,000 millionaires, certainly could afford to pay more tax. In their study of taxation, Jon Kvist and Adrian Sinfield point out, 'The UK Conservative government reduced the top rates of income tax from 83 per cent to 60 per cent as soon as they were elected in 1979, and then again to a single higher rate of 40 per cent in 1988' (1996, p. 22).

Moreover, as the government has not lifted the tax threshold in line with inflation, more and more low earners have been brought into the tax system. The introduction of Value Added Tax and other indirect taxes – which bear proportionately more on those with low incomes – means that the tax system has moved in favour of those with higher incomes. These reforms reveal that large tax changes are possible, although in these instances, in ways which promote inequality. By the same token, a government with different convictions could alter the system to reduce the incomes of those at the top and raise that of those at the bottom. Greater equality is possible within this system.

Kvist and Sinfield also draw attention to another part of taxation, namely what is called 'tax expenditure', a term 'used to cover losses of revenue . . . by granting reliefs and allowances on tax' (p. 13). It is well known that a tax allowance is given for dependent children and Child Benefit is tax-free. The researchers reckon that less attention is given to other reliefs, for instance tax relief on mortgages for home-buyers, exemption from tax on the first £30,000 received on the termination of employment, tax deductible premiums for private health insurance for those aged over sixty, tax deductible contributions to occupational and personal pensions, tax-free income to approved pension funds. They estimate that in 1990, 'tax expenditure' or tax allowances amounted to £51 billion in the UK and that the benefits 'go most generously to those who have most resources and could therefore be regarded as needing them the least' (p. 29).

Lost Revenue

In Britain, it is accepted that millions of pounds of income tax are lost by dishonesty, by tax payers who make false returns. Further, in 1994–5, at least £3.8 million was lost because of VAT under-declarations by companies. In addition, billions of pounds are lost legally through tax loopholes. An incisive article in *The Observer* revealed how it is possible for enormously wealthy financiers to minimize their personal income tax by locating abroad (1995). Rupert Murdoch's companies made a profit of £165 million yet paid no tax at all in the UK. Overall, it is estimated that at least £3 billion, and probably much more, is avoided by financiers in this way.

A society characterized by citizens who regarded each other as neighbours would, as the Bible puts it, 'cheerfully' pay taxes in order to avoid the disadvantages of inequality. Further reform of the 'tax expenditure system', a closure of tax loopholes for the rich, and a stricter application of the law, would reap in many billions of pounds which could be redistributed. Contrary to the wails of the Financial Pessimists, Britain could afford greater equality.

The Wealthy Radicals

Even some who campaign for a reduction in poverty may object to the aim of equality. In 1996, *The Observer Life Magazine* featured the lifestyle of the potential Labour MP, Barbara Follett, who saw nothing amiss in her living in opulence while thousands are in poverty. Members of Labour party governments have led lifestyles akin to that of country gentlemen. They are not alone. The Wealthy Radicals argue that their own privileges are acceptable provided that they are generous to charitable causes and support reforms to alleviate poverty. Indeed, they can positively seethe with indignation about the plight of beggars and the homeless. They want them to be helped – provided that their own superior position is not changed. They do not want equality.

The Nine-Tenths

I must return again to George Lansbury. After initially working with the Liberal party, he decided to throw in his lot with the emerging socialists. The wealthy Liberal MP, Samuel Montagu, made strenuous efforts to stop the talented Lansbury from leaving, and summoned him to an interview which Lansbury recorded as follows,

> I told him I had become a Socialist and wanted to preach social-ism. He replied: 'Don't be silly, I am a Socialist, a better Socialist than you. I give a tenth of my riches each year to the poor.' I said: 'Yes, I know how good you are and respect you more than it is possible to say, but, my dear friend, we Socialists want to prevent you getting the nine-tenths. We do not believe in rich and poor and charity. We want to create wealth and all the means of life and share them equally among the people. (1928, p. 75)

Montagu then offered Lansbury £5 a week until he got a safe Liberal seat in the Commons. Lansbury declined and opted for a job at £1.50 a week where he could remain close to those he wanted to serve.

Radical Harm

As Lansbury implied, the radicals may be sympathetic towards poor people but, by insisting on holding on to their wealth, they do great harm. First, they uphold the great divisions within our society and hence do nothing to change the structures which uphold both inequality and poverty. Second, they perpetuate the system of charity by which the rich demean the poor. Today, the radicals may well call for more generous Income Support levels but, as long as resources are so unfairly distributed, they will con-tinue the system of means-tested benefits which imposes stigma upon recipients. Third, they champion the creed of individual selfishness and thus prevent the spread of the value of mutuality and of the spirit of self-sacrifice for the sake of others. In short, they favour a system based on greed which favours themselves rather than one based on altruism which favours all people. Of course, greedy materialism is a feature of our society. The moral dishonesty of the Wealthy Radicals is that they perpetuate this feature while attempting to give the appearance that they are on the side of the poor.

The 'It's Worse Abroad' Brigade

In discussing the case for lessening inequalities in Britain, I sometimes meet the objection, 'Why bother about Britain? Poverty is far worse in Third World countries, we should just concentrate on the inequalities between us and them.' Undoubtedly, some people in parts of Africa, India and other so-called Third World countries do lack the very essentials of living – food, water, shelter. Undoubtedly, the citizens of affluent countries do have a responsibility to help and, as Paul Vallely shows in his brilliant *Bad Samaritans*, could do so much more sensitively and effectively (1990). But it is not simply a matter of the rich West and the poor Third World. Vast inequalities exist within the latter countries. Palatial homes exist within a few miles of shanty towns; millionaires lives close to hungry people searching rubbish tips. Inequalities have to be tackled within Third World countries as well as between nations.

Inequalities at Home

The plight of people abroad does not excuse the inequalities within Britain – both are wrong. Chris Wigglesworth served as a Church of Scotland minister in the slums of Bombay and then in Africa before returning to Scotland. He wrote,

> I found no incongruity in coming back from Sudan and somehow becoming a Regional Councillor for a ward with too many badly-housed people in it. Many try to play off the poor and powerless of the Third World against the 'relatively deprived' here. 'Of course, you've seen real poverty, people here should be grateful for the welfare state' usually seems to be said by people with private health insurance, over £15,000 a year, a car and their own house . . . . Only a few months of getting to know people in one or two of the euphemistically termed 'difficult-to-let' housing schemes is sufficient to share some experience of lives so lacking in opportunity for change for the better as to be every bit as unacceptable as those of many people in any Indian hutment. (D. Forrester and D. Skene, eds, 1988, p. 10)

As Wigglesworth makes clear, Christians have responsibilities towards people everywhere who suffer from the disadvantages of inequality.

The impact of inequality on those at the bottom end of society is similar whatever the country. Stan and Mari Thekaekara are Indian community workers who have spent much of their lives with the tribal peoples around Gudalur in the Nilgiris Hills south of Mysore. In 1994, they came to Britain and stayed at Moss Side and Hulme in Manchester, St Thomas' in Dudley, and Easterhouse in Glasgow. They soon perceived that the British poor were not starving and wrote,

> Easterhouse was nowhere near one of our tribal villages. Everyone was better housed, clothed and fed. Everyone seemed to have a television, a fridge – some even had cars. All items of luxury for the majority of people in India. But as the week went by we began to see beyond the televisions, refrigerators and cars. Amazingly, similarities between the people of Easterhouse and the Paniyas of the Nilgiris began to emerge. Though the face of poverty was completely different, the impact was exactly the same. (1994, p. 20)

The impact was that those at the bottom end of inequality in both countries suffered worse health, were isolated from the affluent, often felt powerless to alter their circumstances. Those subject to long-term unemployment and poverty could lose enthusiasm for life and motivation for change. In both countries 'The future seemed as bleak and pointless as the present' (p. 20).

Whether between the residents of Britain, whether between the residents of India, whether between those of Britain and India, vast inequalities are wrong and out of line with God's intention for his world. Christians, and others, must not be ready to stand by while human personalities are scarred, while individuality is crushed, while physical and mental ill-health is unnecessarily forced upon citizens. A link has been formed between a few people in Easterhouse and Gudalur. They can learn from each other more effective ways of countering poverty. But the lessons are for us all. That inequalities exist among our kin abroad cannot be an excuse for ignoring the plight of our kin who suffer in Britain.

The Super-Spirituals

Within the Christian Church is an element which thinks that concern with social and material equality is at best irrelevant and at

worst a distraction from the purpose of the Church which is to
save souls, to bring people into a direct relationship with God
and then prepare them for eternity. Martin Luther King illustrated this thinking with the church whose pulpit committee
'listed as the first essential qualification for a new minister: "He
must preach the true gospel and not talk about social issues"'
(1975, p. 131).

The Whole Gospel

Certainly, the Church should be concerned with bringing individuals into a relationship with God. But that is not the whole
gospel. J. A. Motyer, in his scholarly exposition of the book of
Amos, points to the strange words in Amos 5.23, in which God
says to his people, 'Spare me the sound of your songs; I shall not
listen to the strumming of your lutes'. God rejects their worship.
Something must be drastically wrong. The explanation is, as
Motyer puts it, that they have put their religion 'in a box'. They
gathered for spiritual meetings but were ignoring the plight of
the poor and oppressed. He explains the symbolism of some of
the worship, 'The essential meaning of the burnt offering is total
consecration to God: the attitude which holds nothing back . . . .
The essential meaning of the peace offering is fellowship, upward
to God and outward to other folk . . . with special reference to the
helpless, the uncared for' (1974, p. 134). Consecration to God
should have been expressed by obedience to God's command to
love neighbours; fellowship should have been expressed by a oneness, a mutuality, with those who are the unequal. God wants a
people who both worship him and also care for others.

Furthermore, in attending to the material and social needs of
others, Christians are strengthening themselves spiritually. As
Martin Luther King explains, 'We must love our enemies, because
only by loving them can we know God and experience the beauty of
his holiness' (1975, p. 53). God is the God of spiritual and material,
he cares for people's bodies as well as their souls. Hence the
Church must also be concerned about both and concerned not
just for Christians but for all of God's creation. Howard Snyder
puts it well, 'Christians are called to demonstrate God's justice,
mercy and truth toward all people everywhere – not just to our
own kind. Every church should therefore be involved in both
world evangelism and world justice' (1985, p. 41).

Sin First

A variant theme of the Super-Spirituals is to accept that
Christianity should be concerned with social issues but to argue
that, as injustice springs from sin, there is no point in addressing
matters such as poverty and inequality until sin has been tackled.
In other words, convert people then they will behave justly
towards others. In fact, the Super-Spirituals do not apply this
reasoning to all social issues. They are prepared to lobby against
abortion even before the abortionists become Christians. They
do urge the government to uphold Christian family values
amongst all citizens whether they be Christian or not. Strangely,
it is only on matters such as social inequalities that they decide
that the Church should not get involved in politics but should rely
on a strategy of conversion first. Thus they may – rightly in my
view – argue that unborn children are precious before God yet,
once children are born, they do not argue that the children
should have their proper share of this world's goods.

True, we should seek first the kingdom of God, individuals
should strive to discover God. But a part of the kingdom is social
justice. Again, it is the conservative evangelical, J. A. Motyer, who
makes this point so powerfully. He explains that Amos did not
wait for spiritual revival before condemning the affluent for
allowing low wages and other injustices. The nation had to obey
God's commands to care for the needy and then await spiritual
blessing. Motyer concludes, 'We ever want the blessing first and
the duty second, but Amos says that it is those who set themselves
in the way that delights their God who receive life, power and
grace from and in Him' (p. 125).

There are many objectors to equality – the Anti-Levellers, the
Economic Right, the Wealthy Radicals, the 'Its Worse Abroad'
Brigade and the Super-Spirituals. They do make powerful and
popular arguments and in this chapter I have attempted to
counter them on social and economic grounds. A more equal
society need not harm the economy, will not usher in a totalitarian
state. It can be approached by a reformed free market and by state
intervention. It can be afforded. But, in the end, I trace the case
for equality to the Bible, to the life of Christ, to the practices of
the New Testament Church. Dr Martin Luther King is known for
consistently proclaiming racial equality. But he also embraced
social equality and his talks and writings are sermons about a new

society based on equality as expressed in personal attitudes and structural reforms. He wrote, 'disregarding the fact that the gospel deals with man's body as well as with his soul . . . creates a tragic dichotomy between the sacred and the secular. To be worthy of its New Testament origin, the church must seek to transform both individual lives and the social situation that brings to many people anguish of spirit and cruel bondage' (p. 131).

But the New Testament is also about the cross. The supporters of equality will find that some of the opposition to them is so vehement, so heavy, that is almost like a cross that they have to bear.

7

———⚬———

The Cross of Equality

Keir Hardie and Lord Overtoun were both Christians who lived nearly a century ago. Hardie, an illegitimate child raised in poverty, was converted to Christianity, probably at a Moody and Sankey revival meeting. Later he declared, 'the impetus which drove me first of all into the Labour movement . . . has been derived more from the teaching of Jesus of Nazareth than from all other sources combined.' It was as a Christian that he became an egalitarian, campaigning for, as he put it, 'a new order based upon fraternity and justice to all alike' (E. Hughes, ed., 1928, pp. 140, 153). Lord Overtoun, born J. Campbell White, inherited a large chemical works in Glasgow. A zealous member of the Free Church of Scotland, the millionaire gave many donations to Christian causes at home and abroad. He was a frequent speaker and preacher and was on many committees of Christian agencies. He was a strong Sabbatarian, backed the Lord's Day Observance Society and campaigned against Glasgow Corporation for allowing trams to run on Sundays.

In 1899, employees at the chemical works asked *The Labour Leader*, which Hardie edited, to take up their plight. They were working twelve hours a day, without any breaks for food, seven days a week, were liable to horrible skin diseases from the chemicals and, in return, were paid 3d or 4d an hour. Hardie took up his pen. He was enraged at the inequality in which a millionaire who dwelt in a vast mansion paid poverty wages to those who lived in hovels. He wrote, 'Think of it. A human being, made in the image of God, working toilsomely in a hell for four pence an hour' (pp. 85–93). He was disgusted at the hypocrisy, particularly at Overtoun's insistence on Sunday working, and he applied Jesus' condemnation of the Pharisees to him. He asked Lord Overtoun to introduce reforms and called upon other Christian bodies to back his call.

Far from supporting Hardie, Christian ministers – and the secular press – tried to defend Overtoun. As little could be said in his defence, they made attacks upon Hardie. From pulpit and in papers, his writings were dismissed as no more than 'a socialist attack', while Hardie himself was branded as 'an anti-religious atheist'. Hardie retaliated in his columns. He implied that the prosperous Glaswegian citizens had replaced the sacrificial Christianity of the New Testament with a comfortable Christianity which justified their lifestyles and neglected the poor. They wanted the crown of Christianity, but not the cross.

To his credit, Overtoun remained silent and eventually did improve the workers' conditions. The abuse flung at Hardie continued all his life. He was accused of advocating free love, of living in a mansion and having a retinue of servants. The accusations were blatantly untrue – he existed in near poverty – but he could never afford to take legal action against his detractors. He was subject to continued misrepresentation in the press, abuse in public, and when elected to Parliament, he was shunned by many MPs. At meetings he was subjected to ferocious heckling and even stonings. It was the cross he had to bear for promoting principles such as equality. He never changed and was probably satisfied that some small improvements were made and that more followers joined his cause. But his daughter – who wrote that 'All his life he had been subject to a never-ending campaign of abuse and misrepresentation' (p. xi) – considered that his cross, if it can be so called, contributed to his periodic breakdowns in health and his early death.

Conflict

Challenging the Status Quo

Jesus did not anger the Jewish and Roman authorities because he sang hymns or said prayers, not even because he fed the poor. They arrested him and condemned him to death on a cross because he challenged the status quo, because he was a threat to their positions. Of course, Jesus Christ was to die for a reason – the atonement – far beyond the understanding of his enemies and I do not wish to compare today's egalitarians with the divine purpose of the death of Jesus. Nor am I suggesting that they will face the hatred and physical abuse met by Keir Hardie. But there is one similarity: it is that serious challenges to the status quo always meet strong opposition from those who benefit from it.

One reason why the case for equality provokes such a strong response is that it asks the wealthy and powerful to concede some of their privileges. Those who today receive £100,000 or more a year will be angered at the prospect of a reduced income in order that others might have more. Those who are used to being treated as ultra-important may abhor the prospect of a society in which others regard and treat them as equals. This opposition will not only come from those who are most clearly at the top of the ladder of inequality. It will also come from some who are apparently sympathetic towards the socially deprived.

In 1996, Jeremy Paxman and Anna Ford campaigned to allow 'poor children' from the East End of London to have holidays in a posh Oxfordshire village – where some residents were aghast at the prospect. To their credit, they wanted to make life a little better for the poor. But this is not the same as campaigning for a society in which the parents of those children would have the same social advantages as themselves. This is not the same as lessening the physical and geographical distance between themselves and those who live in poverty.

Many of the TV personalities who cheerfully do their bit for Children in Need will not want their salaries reduced so that the parents of needy children do not have to receive help from charities. Indeed, poverty campaigning, drives to improve slightly the fate of those in dire social distress, can be a con which diverts attention away from the case for equality. I have noticed that directors of Social Services Departments and chief executives of national voluntary societies will hear and approve of the youth clubs and family support provided for low-incomed families by the project with which I am associated. But some get very upset if I suggest that they are overpaid and that some of their £60,000–£80,000 salaries could be better spread amongst the same families. The Church of Scotland Report concluded,

> Prosperous and powerful groups usually believe that the status quo is just, and defend their privilege in the name of justice. Society is full of conflicts of interest, and the establishment of justice is rarely possible without conflict. Christians who believe that God has a special care for the poor and weak must

school themselves to rise above their own interests in order to seek God's justice. And doing justice can involve taking sides in conflict in a world that is full of injustice and lovelessness. (D. Forrester and D. Skene, eds, 1988, p. 79)

Those who advocate equality must accept that they are entering into the arena of social conflict.

Another reason why the conflict will be fierce is that egalitarians challenge one of the great sacred cows of our time – the sanctity of the free market system. To repeat, those who advocate equality are not calling for the abolition of all private property. As Richard Tawney stated in *The Acquisitive Society*, 'The idea of some Socialists that private property in land or capital is necessarily mischievous is a piece of scholastic pedantry as absurd as that of those Conservatives who would invest all property with some kind of mysterious sanctity' (1961, p. 82). But the fact is that the unfettered free market leads to enormous and damaging inequalities which are clearly at odds with the teachings of the Bible. This is why the same Tawney asserted, 'If there is one matter on which all Christians should be agreed, it is the duty of doing their utmost to secure that the conditions of a good life are enjoyed by the whole of the rising generation' (1981, p. 179).

Christian egalitarians see the free market not as some 'natural' force which cannot be questioned but as much a creation of human hands as voluntary bodies or state enterprises. They therefore want the market – and the state – to be subjected to human values, via democratic processes, towards a more equal society. Easier said than done. Today it is not just the government which bows the knee to 'the market', but also opposition parties, the major financial institutions and the media. Christians, and others, who therefore question the free market will be opposed by enormous vested interests and will be drawn into conflict in which all the odds are stacked against them.

The advocates of equality, then, may well find themselves in a verbal, social and political battlefield. If this is a part of their cross, then there is another part which consists of the sense of hopelessness they can sometimes feel in the face of the enormity of the opposition. I must admit that the lack of progress in recent decades and the strength of the giants of inequality sometimes depress me. The supporters of equality tend to be the little people. We are not government ministers, have never been inside a London club, do not own newspapers, are not media personalities.

Yet nor was Jesus. Indeed, it was anticipated of him that 'He will not strive, he will not shout, nor will his voice be heard in the streets. He will not snap off a broken reed, nor snuff out a smouldering wick, until he leads justice on to victory' (Matthew 12.19–20, quoting Isaiah 42.2–3). The implication is that if the little people are in the course of God's justice, then they do have sources of strength which are capable of influencing this world. I can think of two sources which are also located in that experience of the cross. One is prayer, the other is expectation and vision.

Prayer

Jesus' life was characterized by prayer yet, as he approached the cross, his prayers intensified. He sweated in prayer in Gethsemane. He prayed on the cross itself. His followers who watched his death knelt in prayer. There were prayers for strength to follow a course of action, prayers for forgiveness for others, prayers of despair, and the great final prayer of victory when Jesus committed himself into God's hands. The cross was about prayer and, as we carry our crosses, we too can be upheld by prayer.

I do not pray enough but I do find a daily diet of prayer to be essential. Prayer has a unifying effect. When Eric Buchanan was the Easterhouse Salvation Army captain, we used to meet at 8.30 a.m. for prayer. We were different kinds of Christians. He considered me too political. I was sometimes uneasy with his aggressive Christianity and rapid-fire conversations. But, in prayer, we grew to understand and love each other.

Prayer also enables us to identify with others. I am not poor, yet in prayer I can stand with those who have been deprived of this world's goods; and in so doing I can be reignited to struggle with them for greater equality.

Prayer is strengthening. It had been a hard week: our local school, where our project holds all its activities, was under threat of closure from the local authority as a part of its programme of cuts. A gang from a nearby area burnt down one of the classrooms. If the school closed then it was difficult to see how our project, which runs activities for over 300 children a week, could continue. Another blow against equality. Then vandals smashed the minibus. I came home thinking, is it worth it? In such moments, I do find that the only recourse is prayer. The only option is to lay it before God. It may sound like pie in the sky but

I do find renewal in prayer. And I hope that Christians will make the achievement of greater equality a part of their daily prayers.

Expectation and Vision

The cross was not the end. Jesus constantly taught that it was a necessary horror, one that would become a gateway to the resurrection. He thus conveyed the expectation that the best was yet to be. Martin Luther King always insisted on expectation even in dark hours. He once admitted that, despite their efforts, black people were 'still confined in an oppressive prison of segregation and discrimination'. He asked,

> Must we respond with bitterness and cynicism? Certainly not. For this will destroy and poison our personalities .... Our most fruitful course is to stand firm with courageous determination, move forward non-violently amid obstacles and setbacks, accept disappointments and cling to hope. Our determined refusal not to be stopped will eventually open the door of fulfilment. (1975, p. 92)

The expectation that change could and would occur thus became a very part of the process which led to reform. Of course, the main theme of this book is not about how Christ defeated sin on the cross. It is not about the struggle for racial equality. But in both of these struggles, hope and expectation played a central part. In like manner, I think that those whose theme is social equality must counter the obstacles of depression and hopelessness by majoring on hope and expectation.

Attention has already been drawn to the fact that social betterment has occurred in Britain, particularly during and immediately after the last War. Change is possible. Again, it is encouraging that equality is being expressed in some neighbourhood groups while the principle of mutuality is being applied by some individuals to their own lives. The expectation must be that equality will be pursued, that the vast inequalities which mar our nation will be reduced. The vision must be upheld if it is to be sought.

I am writing the last chapter of this book. At the same time, I am involved with our local project. The combination of writing about equality and walking amidst inequality drives into me.

I take a couple of youngsters out for a game of pitch and putt. It costs 20p but one only has 15p, it was all his dad and step-mum had. His real mum died in giving birth; his step-mother looks ill and wasted. The other boy was being looked after by his seventeen-year-old sister; his lone mum was working as usual; she works in a café for measly wages. Yesterday I read in the paper of some members of the House of Lords who 'stroll in, have a cup of tea or a drink, listen to question time, often without staying to vote. This qualifies them for a daily allowance of up to £139, plus travel expenses of 47.2p a mile' (Jonathan Steele, 1996). For one day's luxury, they receive more than that woman slaves for in a week. So much for the free market giving people what they deserve. I long for an equal society in which financial abuse is eliminated, in which working parents have a decent income, in which children have similar advantages.

I look at a tenement block which our project is hoping to lease from the council for our clubs and family activities. Our application has only been accepted because it is a 'hard-to-let' property. I remember the families, who were there, showing me the damp, the mould. They have moved but are not much better off. They have no chance of moving to a suburban estate. A friend comes to see me. His flat has been subject to break-ins; he is desperate to move but cannot get rehoused. He asks me to look after his valuables, such as they are, so as to thwart the next set of thieves. A thirteen-year-old boy comes into our project office and dumps a plastic bag on the desk. It contains fifty-two needles he has picked up in his block.

I look at the housing prices in a Sunday magazine. Take your pick in Buckinghamshire: £235,000 for a four-bedroomed cottage in Chalfont St Peter, £179,000 for a three-bedroomed one in Chalfont St Giles, and, if you really are at the bottom end of the market, £104,500 for a two-up, two-down. All with large gardens, near grammar schools, tennis and golf clubs. The estate agents even point to Gold Hill Baptist Church which 'draws visitors [and their cars] from far and wide'. There is little crime. Residents smilingly point out that living here improves your chances of still having wheels on your Range Rover in the morning.

I long for a society which is not fragmented, in which crime is low because people value each other. I long for a society in which all people will have dry rooms, adequate space, stairs without needles on them, a garden. I long for a society in which those, who at present can spend £235,000 on their homes, are so filled with the spirit of mutuality that they will take less so that others can have more.

We are at camp in Norfolk. My wife Annette asks me the name

of one of our thirteen-year-olds who has legs like sticks. He has already been nicknamed Kes. He is smaller than the ten-year-olds from Eastbourne. He will probably suffer more illnesses than them in his lifetime and almost certainly that lifetime will be shorter. I want a society where the accidents of birth will not immediately place some children at far greater risk of ill-health, handicap, early death. I want the best possible health for all.

A seventeen-year-old girl comes to our flat and tells my wife and me that she has become a Christian. She is one of a large family. She is beginning to help in the youth clubs and has potential but needs more confidence. She is unemployed but would like a job working with young children. Annette explains some of the options. The chances are not good. I rejoice that she has entered into a personal relationship with God. A part of equality is that the gospel reaches young people on the estates and in the inner cities as much as in Buckinghamshire and on the south coast. But the whole gospel is that God cares for that girl materially and socially as well as spiritually.

I long for a society in which those social disadvantages – which make it difficult for her to obtain employment, which mean that her personal development is hindered – are removed. It can be done. Years ago, Sydney and Beatrice Webb explained that our nation was characterized by the extremes of affluence and poverty because it 'deliberately chooses inequality' (M. Desai, ed., 1995, p. 172). In the future it is possible for it to deliberately choose the pursuit of equality.

But we as individuals are a part of that nation. Therefore, I believe that now we must demonstrate that equality by breaking the evil of inequality. In so doing we may have to carry crosses – emotional, social, physical crosses – of our own. So be it. Yet just as Christ's coming amongst the needy was associated with joy, so today we will also experience the warmth, the friendship, the mutuality, of joining others who struggle for the same end.

Bibliography

Abel-Smith, B. and P. Townsend, *The Poor and the Poorest*. Codicote Press 1965.

Alton, D., 'Stopping the rot' (*Third Way*, June 1994).

Archbishop of Canterbury's Commission on Urban Priority Areas, *Faith in the City*, Church House Publishing 1985.

Anderson, D., ed., *The Kindness that Kills*. SPCK 1984.

Atkinson, D., *The Common Sense of Community*. Demos 1994.

Balls, E., 'Tide is turning in attitudes to inequality' (*The Guardian*, 29 July 1996).

Barclay, Sir P. (chair), *The Inquiry Into Income and Wealth*. Joseph Rowntree Foundation 1995.

Bayley, M., *Welfare: a moral issue*. Diocese of Sheffield Social Responsibility Committee 1989.

Bebbington, A. and J. Miles, 'The background of children who enter local authority care' (*British Journal of Social Work*, Vol. 19, October 1989).

Becker, S. and S. MacPherson, *Poor Clients*. University of Nottingham 1986.

Boswell, J., ed., *What Justice Demands*. Christian Socialist Movement 1995.

Bradshaw, J. and H. Holmes, *Living on the Edge*. Child Poverty Action Group (CPAG) 1989.

Bradshaw, J. and J. Morgan, 'Budgeting on benefit' (*New Society*, 6 March 1987).

Brockway, F., *Bermondsey Story: the life of Alfred Salter*. Allen and Unwin 1951.

Brown, G., 'In the real world' (*The Guardian*, 2 August 1996).

Bryant, C., *Possible Dreams*. Hodder and Stoughton 1996.

Cantacuzino, M., 'For whom the bell tolled' (*The Guardian*, 16 July 1996).

Carey, G., *The Gates of Glory*. Hodder and Stoughton 1992.

Cohen, R., et al., *Hardship Britain*. Child Poverty Action Group (CPAG) and Family Service Units (FSU) 1992.

Colton, M., et al., *Stigma and Social Welfare*. Avebury 1997.

Condon, T., 'Lifestyles: Sir Gavin Laird' (*Scotland on Sunday*, 26 May 1996).

Lord Dahrendorf (chair), *Commission on Wealth Creation and Social Cohesion*, Liberal Democrat Party 1995.

Desai, M., ed., *LSE on Equality*. London School of Economics (LSE) Books 1995.

Desai, M., 'Equality: the debate goes on' (*LSE Magazine*, Summer 1996).

Drabble, M., *The Case for Equality*. Fabian Society 1988.

Ferguson, R., *Geoff*. Famedram Publishing 1979.

Field, F., *Unequal Britain*. Arrow Books 1974.

Field, F., *Making Welfare Work*. Institute of Community Studies 1995.

Field, F., J. Gray, W. Hutton, J. King and D. Marquand, 'This is what we mean' (*The Observer*, 7 July 1996).

Forrester, D. and D. Skene, eds, *Just Sharing: a Christian approach to the distribution of wealth, income and benefits*. Epworth Press 1988.

Friedman, M., *Capitalism and Freedom*. University of Chicago Press 1962.

George V. and I. Howards, *Poverty Amidst Affluence*. Edward Elgar 1991.

Gerrard, N., 'The workaholics' (*The Observer*, 28 July 1996).

Gibbons, J., et al., *Family Support and Prevention*. HMSO 1990.

Glasgow Director of Public Health, *Annual Report, 1991–2*. Greater Glasgow Health Board 1993.

Golding P. and S. Middleton, *Images of Welfare*. Blackwell and Robertson 1982.

Gray, J., 'Yes it hurt – but it just didn't work' (*The Guardian*, 20 August 1996).

Hattersley, R., 'Balance of power' (*The Guardian*, 25 July 1996).

Hayek, F., *The Road to Serfdom*. Routledge and Kegan Paul 1944.

Heywood, J., *Children in Care*. Routledge and Kegan Paul 1959.

Holman, B., *Good Old George: the life of George Lansbury*. Lion Publishing 1990.

Holman, B., *A New Deal for Social Welfare*. Lion Publishing 1993.

Holman, B., 'Shaken not heard' (*The Guardian*, 22 January 1994).

Holman, B., 'Prophet motive: interview with Jim Wallis' (*Third Way*, July 1995).

Holman, B., *The Corporate Parent: Manchester Children's Department 1948-71*. National Institute for Social Work 1996.

Holman, B., *FARE Dealing*. Community Development Foundation 1997.

Holtermann, S., *All Our Futures*. Barnardos 1995.

Hughes, E., ed., *Keir Hardie's Speeches and Writings*. Forward Printing and Publishing Company 1928.

Hutton, W., 'The real price of poverty' (*The Guardian*, 24 February 1992).

Hutton, W., 'Why the rich must be forced to hand over their vast inheritance' (*The Guardian*, 8 August 1994).

Hutton, W., 'Why the poor remain silent' (*The Guardian*, 13 February 1995).

Hutton, W., 'A state of decay' (*The Guardian*, 18 September 1995).

Hutton, W., *The State We're In*. Jonathan Cape 1995.

Irvine, C., 'The real voice of poverty' (*The Guardian*, 14 December 1988).

Joseph, Sir K. and J. Sumption, *Equality*. John Murray 1979.

Keegan, V., 'Highway robbery by the super-rich' (*The Guardian*, 22 July 1996).

Kirkwood, D., cited in *The Guardian*, 15 November 1995.

Knight, B., *Voluntary Action*. Centris 1993.

Kumar, V., *Poverty and Inequality in the UK: the effects on children*. National Children's Bureau 1993.

Kvist, J. and A. Sinfield, *Comparing Tax Routes in Denmark and the UK*. Danish National Institute of Social Research 1996.

Lansbury, G., *My Life*. Constable 1928.

Lansbury, G., *My England*. Selwyn and Blound 1934.

Le Grand, J., *The Strategy for Equality*. Allen and Unwin 1982.

Lister, R., *The Exclusive Society: citizenship and the poor*. Child Poverty Action Group (CPAG) 1990.

Lupton, R., *Return Flight*. Family Consultation Service (FCS) Urban Ministries 1993.

Luther King, M., *Strength to Love*. Fontana 1975.

Mack, J. and S. Lansley, *Poor Britain*. Allen and Unwin 1985.

Marshall, T. H., *Social Policy*. Hutchinson 1965.

Mayo, B., *Gospel Exploded: reaching the unreached*. Triangle 1996.

Mayor, S., *The Churches and the Labour Movement*. Independent Press 1967.

McLellan N. and C. Flecknoe, *Neighbourhood Community Development*. McLellan and Flecknoe 1992.

Mills, H. and M. Bright, 'Poverty makes children shorter' (*The Observer*, 11 August 1996).

Motyer, J. A., *The Message of Amos*. Inter-Varsity Press 1974.

Murray, C., *The Emerging British Underclass*. Institute of Economic Affairs 1990.

National Children's Home, *Poverty and Nutrition Survey* 1991.

Nolan, C., 'A crying shame' (*The Guardian*, 22 May 1996).

Oppenheim, C. and L. Hawker, *Poverty: the Facts*. Child Poverty Action Group (CPAG) 1996.

Pacione, M., *Glasgow*. Wiley 1995.

Paxman, J., *Friends in High Places: who rules Britain?* Penguin 1991.

Rawls, J., *A Theory of Justice*. Oxford University Press 1972.

Rhodes, L. and J. Viet Wilson, *The Family Experience of Children Coming Into Care in Newcastle Local Authority, 1971–7*. Mimeograph 1978.

Russell, H., *Poverty Close to Home*. Mowbray 1995.

Scott, T., *Glimpses of Hope*. Unpublished 1994.

Sheppard, D., cited in *The Guardian*, 15 November 1995.

Smith, D., ed., *Understanding the Underclass*. Policy Studies Institute 1992.

Smith, R., 'Unemployment: here we go again' (*British Medical Journal*, Vol. 302, 1991).

Snyder, H., *Kingdom Lifestyle*. Marshall Pickering 1985.

Social Justice Commission, *Social Justice: strategies for national renewal* Vintage 1994.

Steele, J., 'Labour out for blood over the peers' (*The Observer*, 28 July 1996).

Stott, J., *The Cross of Christ*. Inter-Varsity Press 1986.

Stott, J., *The Message of Ephesians: God's new society*. Inter-Varsity Press 1994.

Tawney, R. H., *Equality*. Allen and Unwin 1938.

Tawney, R. H., *The Acquisitive Society*. Fontana 1961.

Tawney, R. H., *The Attack and Other Papers*. Allen and Unwin 1981.

Terrill, R., *R. H. Tawney and His Times*. Andre Deutsch 1974.

Thekaekara, S. and M., *Across the Geographical Divide*. Centre for Innovation in Voluntary Action 1994.

Townsend, P., *The Social Minority*. Allen Lane 1973.

Urwin, E. and D. Wollen, eds, *John Wesley, Christian Citizen: selections from his social teaching*. Epworth Press 1937.

Vallely, B. ed., *What Women Want*. Virago 1996.

Vallely, P., *Bad Samaritans*. Hodder and Stoughton 1990.

Vincent, D., *Poor Citizens*. Longman 1991.

Wallis, J., *The New Radical*. Lion Publishing 1983.

Wallis, J., *The Soul of Politics*. Fount 1995.

Walter, T., *Basic Income*. Boyars 1989.

Weir, A., 'Act of duty' (*Community Care*, 25–31 July 1996).

Whelan, R., *The Corrosion of Charity*. Institute of Economic Affairs 1996.

Whitehead, M., ed., *The Health Divide*. Health Educational Council 1987.

Wilkinson, R., 'Income distribution and life expectancy' (*British Medical Journal*, Vol. 304, 1992).

Wilkinson, R., *Unfair Shares*. Barnardos 1994.

Wilkinson, R., *Unhealthy Societies*. Routledge and Kegan Paul 1996.

Wilson, H. and G. Herbert, *Parents and Children in the Inner City*. Routledge and Kegan Paul 1978.

Wootton, B., *Incomes Policy: an inquest and a proposal*. Davies-Poynter 1974.

Wootton, B., *In Pursuit of Equality*. Fabian Society 1976.

Other material used from *The Guardian*, 4 April, 14, 26, 28 June 1996; *The Daily Mail*, 2 October 1995; *The Observer*, 24 September 1995; *The Observer Life Magazine*, 28 July 1996.

The Society for Promoting Christian Knowledge (SPCK) has as its purpose three main tasks:

- **Communicating the Christian faith in its rich diversity**
- **Helping people to understand the Christian faith and to develop their personal faith**
- **Equipping Christians for mission and ministry**

SPCK Worldwide serves the Church through Christian literature and communication projects in over 100 countries. Special schemes also provide books for those training for ministry in many parts of the developing world. SPCK Worldwide's ministry involves Churches of many traditions. This worldwide service depends upon the generosity of others and all gifts are spent wholly on ministry programmes, without deductions.

SPCK Bookshops support the life of the Christian community by making available a full range of Christian literature and other resources, and by providing support to bookstalls and book agents throughout the UK. SPCK Bookshops' mail order department meets the needs of overseas customers and those unable to have access to local bookshops.

SPCK Publishing produces Christian books and resources, covering a wide range of inspirational, pastoral, practical and academic subjects. Authors are drawn from many different Christian traditions, and publications aim to meet the needs of a wide variety of readers in the UK and throughout the world.

The Society does not necessarily endorse the individual views contained in its publications, but hopes they stimulate readers to think about and further develop their Christian faith.

For further information about the Society, please write to:
SPCK, Holy Trinity Church, Marylebone Road,
London NW1 4DU, United Kingdom.